# Tournament Management

# TOURNAMENT MANAGEMENT

A Superintendent's Guide to Preparing a Golf Course for Competition

John C. Miller, CGCS

 John Wiley & Sons, Inc.

Copyright © 2009 by John Wiley & Sons, Inc. All rights reserved

Published by John Wiley & Sons, Inc., Hoboken, New Jersey
Published simultaneously in Canada

Limit of Liability/Disclaimer of Warranty: While the publisher and the author have used their best efforts in preparing this book, they make no representations or warranties with respect to the accuracy or completeness of the contents of this book and specifically disclaim any implied warranties of merchantability or fitness for a particular purpose. No warranty may be created or extended by sales representatives or written sales materials. The advice and strategies contained herein may not be suitable for your situation. You should consult with a professional where appropriate. Neither the publisher nor the author shall be liable for any loss of profit or any other commercial damages, including but not limited to special, incidental, consequential, or other damages.

For general information about our other products and services, please contact our Customer Care Department within the United States at (800) 762-2974, outside the United States at (317) 572-3993 or fax (317) 572-4002.

Wiley also publishes its books in a variety of electronic formats. Some content that appears in print may not be available in electronic books. For more information about Wiley products, visit our web site at www.wiley.com.

*Library of Congress Cataloging-in-Publication Data:*

Miller, John C.

Tournament management: a superintendent's guide to preparing a golf course for competition/ John C. Miller.

    p.  cm.

  Includes index.

  ISBN 978-0-470-19228-3 (cloth)

  1. Golf courses—Maintenance. 2. Turf management. 3. Golf courses—Environmental aspects. 4. Golf course managers—Handbooks, manuals, etc. I. Title.

GV975.5.M43 2009

796.352'069–dc22

2008019005

Printed in the United States of America

10 9 8 7 6 5 4 3 2 1

*To my wife, Gail, and my son, Brandon, for their patience and understanding during the long hours and sacrifices they have endured so that I could do the one thing I have a passion for: being a golf course superintendent. Also to my mother and father, for all of their support and encouragement over the years. And last, but not least, to the spouses of golf course superintendents everywhere who sacrifice so that they can do their job.*

# CONTENTS

# FOREWORD

Since the days of Old Tom Morris, golf course maintenance has been a mystical blend of art and science. The greenkeeper or superintendent is called upon to use his powers of observation and intuition of things to come to most effectively and efficiently apply his knowledge, skill, and available resources to grow healthy turf. It is comparable to a friendly chess game played against Mother Nature: She has control of the weather and pests, and the superintendent must anticipate her moves and defend against them. The winner is determined by the golfers, based on whether the playing surfaces of the golf course meet or exceed their expectations.

When the profession was in its infancy, 150 years ago, the greenkeeper had few tools or resources to work with, so his ability to win the golfer's favor was much more art than science. As turfgrass science evolved over the past century, an increasing emphasis was placed on the science, and less on the art, of green-keeping. Today, the pendulum is shifting again, in response to an environmental reawakening and a focus on resource conserva-tion; once again, the art of golf course grooming is becoming more important. Unfortunately, while the science of turfgrass has been well documented, the artful side has not. That makes John Miller's timely book an invaluable source of information, which is not taught in school.

I have been privileged to know John from the time he was a young greenkeeper at the London Country Club, a small rural country club in Ohio, where my mom and dad were members. I played the course there often, and my background in golf course management enabled me to observe and judge who was winning the golf course chess game, Mother Nature or the greens staff. After John completed his formal education and became the golf course superintendent of the club, I continued to observe the contest, and I marveled at how often John emerged victorious, even with few resources at his disposal. In retrospect, I now realize that John was mastering the *art* of greenkeeping.

As John's professional stature grew, and he moved up the career ladder to better funded and resourced jobs in Ohio, he never forgot the lessons of his early years. Today, as the first tour agronomist for the Ladies Professional Golfers Association (LPGA), he is able to share his knowledge, experience, and art with his fellow superintendents when he visits and consults for tournament venues across North America. And now he has expanded his reach by taking the time to write this book and codify his knowledge and insights.

*Tournament Management: A Superintendent's Guide to Preparing a Golf Course for Competition* was not written only for high-budget tour stops, but to assist all superintendents and greenkeepers, regardless of their available resources. Remember, this is the artful side of golf course maintenance, and as in Old Tom's day, the less you have to work with the more artful you need to be.

I trust that you will find John's book as interesting as it is helpful. That is the spirit in which it was written. It is this willingness among practitioners to share information that has made golf course maintenance such a great profession and industry to work in today.

Michael J. Hurdzan, PhD
Hurdzan/Fry Environmental Golf Course Design
American Society of Golf Course Architects

# TOURNAMENT MANAGEMENT

# CHAPTER ONE

# PLANNING AND COMMUNICATION

*Perfection is not attainable. But if we chase perfection, we can catch excellence.*
—VINCE LOMBARDI

All golf courses and clubs host tournaments. Many are put on for club members or regular golfers at the local public golf course; others are hosted by the golf course and run by professional organizations. These tournaments may take on a variety of formats, from club championships and member-guest outings to state and professional tournaments. But no matter what the format or the venue of these tournaments, a detailed and well-thought-out plan is essential to their successful outcome.

No golf course superintendent, no matter how skilled in the art and science of greens management, can effectively implement a tournament plan without the cooperation of all the tournament stakeholders. Thus, the first step in the planning process must be to identify these people.

## IDENTIFYING STAKEHOLDERS

Start by making a list of everyone who will be involved with your event, all those you will need to communicate with throughout plan implementation. This list may contain some or all of the following:

- Owner of the course/club
- Board of directors, board president

- Greens chairperson
- General manager
- Director of golf
- Golf professional
- Food and beverage director
- Tournament chairperson/committee chairs
- Assistant golf course superintendent
- Full-time and seasonal maintenance staff

With that list in hand, you can begin to gather information from each of those individuals.

## SOLICITING INPUT

Solicit input from everyone who will be involved in the tournament, to ensure that you have all the information you will need to carry out each and every aspect of your plan, effectively and efficiently. The information you seek will, of course, vary depending on the source. For example:

- Your golf professional will tell you the basic parameters of the tournament—the date of the event, the number of people playing, the type of golfers, and how the course should be set up.
- The food and beverage director will provide you with a list of possible food stations that will need to be set up to accommodate the golfers and spectators.
- The club manager will inform you about any contracts that have been signed, and explain the details of the agreements that have been reached with the companies, and how this will affect the course and the tournament.
- Committee members (described in the next section) will itemize the expectations of golfers or members for the tournament.
- The assistant superintendent and the maintenance staff will update you about current conditions and any problems on the course, as well as offer their perspective as to what needs to be done to meet the needs of the other parties.

Once you are sure you have left no one out of your information-gathering process, take that information and start putting it into useful, and usable, form. You might want to start by combining any areas that overlap or deal with generally the same issues or situations, to avoid duplication of effort. Once you have honed these areas, you can begin to establish committees.

## ESTABLISHING COMMITTEES

Tournament committees will be composed of the people who have relevant knowledge in each of the areas you delineated in the information-gathering phase, those whose help will be critical to making the tournament successful. Tournament committees typically cover the following areas:

* Scoring
* Security
* Player Registration
* Construction (this includes skyboxes, bleachers, roping and staking the golf course; this area heavily involves the golf course superintendent)
* Traffic and Parking
* Communications
* Media

Be sure everyone is onboard before scheduling a first meeting with these groups, at which time they will identify their specific goals and objectives.

You, as golf course superintendent, need not be present at every committee meeting; but it is your responsibility to communicate on a regular basis with the chairs of each committee to ensure they are addressing their assigned objectives, and in a timely fashion.

The information you will need from these meetings should answer such questions as:

* What is the caliber of golfer playing in the event?
* How many golfers will there be?
* How many days will the tournament and any practice rounds last?
* What will be the schedule for the tournament (including start time and type of start, e.g., #1 tee, #1 and #10 tees, shotgun, etc.)?

- What time will the maintenance staff be able to return to the course if evening maintenance is required?
- Will spectators be permitted to view the event?
- Will there be outside vendors setting up; and, if so, what will they display? What will their power requirements be?
- Will portable restrooms be needed? If so, how many, and where will they be located?

As you are compiling this information, it's a good idea to generate checklists or action plans, detailing from start to finish who has been assigned to each task—from initial contact to on-site delivery of goods or services to cleanup and removal of the items.

## LONG-TERM PREPARATION STRATEGY

Your planning process must begin months or, in some instances, years in advance, depending on the scope of the event. You will want to take a comprehensive inventory of your entire operation, to include your staff (number and individual capabilities); equipment (type and condition); maintenance facility; the course itself; and, most importantly, turf conditions, safety issues, logistics, and staging of operations.

Here are some general guidelines that every golf course superintendent will need to focus on from a long-term perspective:

1. Start no later than one year before the event.
2. Schedule regular planning meetings with all golf course staff and management.
3. Generate an equipment inventory.
4. Take an inventory of the entire operation.
5. Determine staffing requirements.
6. Review the golf course from a competitive standpoint, and make necessary changes.
7. Establish tournament conditioning goals.
8. Adjust the agronomic program to resolve any long-term problems for growing healthy turfgrass (see Chapter Two).
9. Develop a tournament budget line-item.
10. Conduct a trial run.

## Evaluating the Maintenance Facility

A good place to start is by taking a good, hard look at your maintenance facility. Is it spacious enough outside? Depending on the type of tournament your club/course is hosting, you may be required to bring in extra equipment, additional personnel, or extra materials, so you will need as much space as you can possibly get. Inside storage space is just as important. Depending on the location and security of your maintenance compound, you will want to store as much equipment inside as possible, for security purposes. Nothing can ruin a tournament faster than vandals intent on stealing or damaging the equipment, costing you time and money.

Next, check out the repair shop. Is it well equipped? Do you have all you need to keep your equipment running properly? Do you have on hand the equipment necessary to make quick repairs during the tournament, to ensure smooth operations? Consider such items as rapid reel grinders, hoist and lift tables, adequate tools and tool storage, good lighting, and a spacious, well-organized workspace.

Then move on to your chemical storage and mixing facility. Depending on the type of event, you may be hosting spectators, the media, club officials, and guests at your maintenance facility. You want to make sure that everything is up to code, clean, neat, and safe.

## Evaluating Equipment Needs

The main question to ask here is, do you have enough equipment on hand to ensure a successful tournament? To answer this:

1. Itemize the jobs that need to be done and the time frame in which they must be accomplished.
2. Identify the equipment needed to complete each one.
3. Review your equipment inventory in terms of how you want to condition the golf course for your tournament. How much additional equipment might you need? Where will you get it?
4. Identify any missing pieces and start calling vendors to find those who might be willing to loan them to you. If you cannot

make appropriate arrangements with vendors, contact other local golf course superintendents and ask if it would be possible to borrow the necessary items for the duration of your event. Determine whether any of your equipment needs replacement, and how much it will cost (see the sidebar, "Budgeting for Equipment Replacement").

While you are doing your equipment inventory, don't forget to check the condition of each piece. Make sure it's all up to date and in good running order—even if it is only going to be used as backup.

## BUDGETING FOR EQUIPMENT REPLACEMENT

Here's a good rule of thumb to follow in regard to equipment replacement and your capital budget: your annual capital expenditures for equipment should be approximately 10 percent of the total value of all of your equipment. For example, if the total value of all of your maintenance equipment is $1 million, your annual capital expenditure on equipment purchases should be $100,000 per year.

An efficient way to keep track of your equipment is to create a spreadsheet that lists each piece of equipment, its purchase date and purchase price, the expected replacement date and price, and its serial number (see Table 1.1). Using this type of inventory checklist makes it easy to stay current, as well as to prepare a five-year capital improvement plan.

TABLE 1.1. EQUIPMENT INVENTORY SPREADSHEET

| Item | Purchase Date | Purchase Price | Replacement Date | Expected Replacement Price | Serial Number |
|------|---------|---------|-------------|-------------|--------|
| Toro Grn Mwr | 3/10/04 | $ 4,200 | 3/2011 | $ 5,000 | 12687 |
| Jac. Triplex | 4/3/05 | $18,000 | 4/2010 | $21,000 | J2309 |
| JD Tractor | 2/10/96 | $26,000 | 2/2011 | $37,500 | JD33210 |

Your equipment inventory must also take into account the tasks you will need to perform each day to prepare the golf course for the tournament along with the time frame in which these tasks must be completed. Assume, for example, you have two fairway mowers, and that it takes your staff eight hours to mow fairways. Now assume the tournament has an 8:00 a.m. shotgun start and you plan to mow the fairways prior to play. In this case, you will need two additional fairway mowers.

Don't underestimate the importance of utility vehicles. They will be used to transport your staff as they go about their daily tasks, as well as to take care of all of the extra chores that inevitably arise as the tournament date nears. Likewise, consider whether the facility will need to accommodate outside groups that will, for example, be putting up tents or setting up staffing areas around the golf course. If so, these people will also need carts for transport. Bottom line: Be sure to have an adequate number of utility vehicles on hand for both staff and tournament committee participants.

## Evaluating Staffing Needs

At the same time you are evaluating your equipment needs, you should do the same for staffing. Think about the number and type of tasks that will need to be done to meet the goals that have been set forth for your event. Do you have enough personnel to achieve those goals? If the answer is no, where will you get the additional help? Again, consider contacting local course superintendents to see if they might be willing to send members of their staff to your facility for the morning or the evening maintenance routines, for example. If this is not possible, you need to know well in advance of the event so that you can hire the staff you need through staffing agencies and/or enlist the help of volunteers.

If you will be counting on volunteer assistance, don't wait to create a sign-up form and distribute it. Hand it out at chapter meetings, email it to golf course superintendents and industry members, and post it anywhere it is likely to be seen. Include on this form the dates of the tournament, available shifts and the time of those shifts, the number of people you need for the shifts, and any other pertinent information.

Once you have your temporary staff lined up, whether volunteers or employees from other golf courses, it's critical that you set up informational meetings with them. To best match these "temps" to tasks, and to ensure full-task coverage, at the first meeting, ask them to fill out a background information sheet, on which they should be asked to describe their availability (days and times) and their capabilities. Make sure, as well, to get detailed contact information from them. You want to be able to reach them at a moment's notice for any number of reasons, such as if weather will cause a delay or cancellation to tournament play, or if you find yourself short-handed at the last minute. (Email is very effective for this type of communication.)

At a subsequent meeting, it's your turn to distribute information to your volunteers and "borrowed" employees. Start with the basics, including clear directions to your golf course and start times for morning and afternoon schedules. Then pass out individual assignments—the days and times each volunteer will be working and their specific tasks. As a courtesy, distribute a list of everyone's contact information, in case people want to carpool to the event.

## CONDUCTING A GOLF COURSE INVENTORY

You will need ample time to conduct the golf course inventory. Begin by traveling around the golf course; stand on each tee and in the landing areas, and imagine the shot from the player's point of view. Ask yourself:

* Will the player not see any hazards lurking at the edge of the fairway or green?
* If there is a hazard in front of the tee or bisecting the fairway, has the vegetation grown up so much that the player will not be able to see the golf ball land?

If the answer to either of these questions is yes, begin now to plan the necessary steps needed to correct the situation.

As you travel the golf course, check out the boundary markers; make sure that both the rules officials and players can see from stake to stake, and that the vegetation between stakes has been trimmed. Make a final trim of the boundary areas approximately 10 days to 2 weeks prior to the event, so that if the boundaries are to be painted, this can be done after the areas have been trimmed for the last time prior to the event.

Likewise, inventory your greens, tees, fairways, roughs, and bunkers, and make notes of anything that is not tournament-ready. (Note: Tees, fairways, roughs, and bunkers are covered in detail in Chapters Four and Five.) Of primary importance is to identify dangerous trees, any areas that might need to be protected from spectator traffic, and other growth that may need to be trimmed (see Figure 1.1).

Focus on young trees that may be staked or have guy wires supporting them. If the wires or stakes cannot be removed, you may want to work with rules officials to establish a policy for addressing the situation when a golf ball enters the area where the

FIGURE 1.1. DURING THE GOLF COURSE INVENTORY, IDENTIFY AREAS THAT NEED TO BE TRIMMED. IN THIS PICTURE, NOTICE THE BUNKER ON THE LEFT THAT WOULD BE HIDDEN IF THE TREES WERE NOT TRIMMED BACK.

## PLAY GOLF WITH YOUR PROFESSIONAL

As part of the early preparation of the golf course, it's important to review the course from a competitive standpoint. The best way to get that point of view is to ask your golf professional to join you for a round of golf; invite members of the tournament and rules committees to join your party, as well. Ask this group for input on such points as:

- Potential hole locations for the event
- How the bunkers play
- Which teeing areas might be used for the competition
- Width of the fairways—are they too wide or too narrow?
- Target green speed

Make sure everyone looks at the hazard areas, and discusses the way the golf course is currently marked, to identify potential areas of concern. Other topics to cover include: appropriate height of the rough for the competition, caliber of player, and cart policy for the event. Throughout these discussions, take notes, so that later you can prioritize the issues that have been raised and begin working toward solutions as soon as possible.

stakes or wires are located. By taking the time to address this issue well in advance of the tournament, you can ensure correct rulings will be made during play, and that your markings will have a professional rules official input to back up the decision, if necessary.

Tree work, in general, must be done well ahead of the tournament date. This is one of the reasons you must start the planning and preparation as much as one year in advance. When the tournament date draws nearer, you want to be able to spend your time concentrating on preparing the golf course—on the agronomics and fine-tuning of the turfgrass. Here are a number of action steps to take when it comes to addressing tree work:

- Survey any damaged trees for safety and presentation.
- Remove any low-hanging branches that may interfere with maintenance operations, gallery viewing, or play.

- If you mulch around the trees on the golf course, level the mulch rings so that a golfer can play the shot if the ball comes to rest atop of the mulched area.
- If you decide an area needs to be improved by adding a tree or group of trees, do this early. Ideally, solicit the advice of a golf course architect, and have the tournament rules committee review the planting location or locations. Make sure you allow room for future growth, so it does not impede on the playability of the hole.

Another important aspect of your golf course strategy is to start correcting any long-term agronomic problems, which may include shade issues, poor drainage, excessive thatch, or any area where top-quality turf has been difficult to establish. In these areas, determine the true cause of the problem and look for permanent solutions. You may need to call in experts to help you with this; and, subsequently, you may have to "sell the cure" to your board of directors or owners. Clearly, this must be addressed early in the tournament preparation process so that any sod that needs to be installed, or seed that needs to be planted, will have time to root properly and mature by tournament time. (Details on implementing an effective agronomics plan are forthcoming in Chapter Two.)

## Scheduling Maintenance and Communicating with Members

As the new golf season approaches, fill in the dates of important maintenance functions on the master calendar. Try to schedule tasks such as aerification when the weather is most conducive to recovery of the turf, to minimize the time that play is disrupted (Figure 1.2). Don't forget to allot time for educating management staff, committee members, and, eventually, the golfers, as to the benefits of these important tasks. It is vital to running a quality operation that everyone be on the same page, so that consistent information is passed on to golfers and members about events happening on the golf course.

There are a number of effective ways to communicate maintenance operations to the appropriate recipients:

Figure 1.2. Put Aerification Dates on the Golf Course Master Schedule Before Adding Anything Else.

- Give management staff this information during staff meetings, at which time they should be encouraged to ask questions to ensure they understand the maintenance procedures taking place on the golf course.
- Submit an announcement to the golf course newsletter.
- Post a memo on the club bulletin board and in the men's and women's locker rooms.
- Make a presentation at a board meeting or at a members meeting; these are ideal venues for reaching a large number of important stakeholders at the same time. After your presentation, open the floor to question-and-answer sessions, to assure clarity.

Be sure to take advantage of technology for your communications. Applications such as PowerPoint are easy to learn, and make it possible to quickly produce professional-looking presentations. Don't forget to include pictures—remember, a picture is worth a thousand words.

---

## NOTE

Inevitably, as soon as you have entered maintenance dates onto the club calendar, someone will ask you to move them, to accommodate an outing or golf event. As often as possible, stand firm! Remember, you chose these dates to produce optimum turf growth and recovery for the tournament. That said, on occasion, you'll have no choice but to reschedule. For example, the club may book an outing in order to earn a substantial fee, in which case the financial health of the club will take temporary precedence over the health of the turf. The point is, be flexible, but never lose sight of your primary objective: to produce top-quality turf and, ultimately, a successful tournament.

---

### *Work Backward to Achieve Maintenance Goals*

With the date of the tournament determined, you can start planning your maintenance strategy so that the golf course will be in peak condition by that date. The best way to achieve this is to work backward. Say, for example, your maintenance strategy to produce smooth, rolling greens is to topdress every 10 days during the season. Take out your calendar, find your tournament date, decide when you want to make the last topdressing application prior to the tournament (usually five to seven days prior), and count backward every 10 days to arrive at your topdressing dates. Do the same for spraying and fertilization applications.

Using this tactic will also help you to schedule such jobs as spot treating of chemicals on weeds, such as *poa annua,* or sodding certain areas and allowing for recovery (Figure 1.3). You know from experience that during certain times of year and weather conditions, sod will heal very quickly; conversely, if done when conditions are not ideal, it will take much longer. The same is true in areas that have been treated chemically for removal of weeds. The dead area will take time to heal; and if it happens to be on a green, it may even need to be removed with a cup cutter and require the installation of a new plug to reduce the healing window.

Figure 1.3. *Poa Annua* Eradication Using Finale Herbicide Would Need to Take Place Well in Advance of Any Tournament.

This technique is also valuable when it comes to planting flowers. If you plan to use flowers around the club house or the golf course to meet a certain design intent, you will need to determine when to plant the flowers to meet those goals. This can be especially challenging if your tournament is in early spring or late fall.

## Identifying Tournament-Specific Conditioning Goals

No aspect of the tournament planning process is more important than conditioning the course for the event. The first step is to outline those goals, which should be done in conjunction with course officials. Do not move forward until all interested parties have signed on. Without their agreement and cooperation, it will be impossible to get the golf course in peak condition for the event.

In setting your tournament conditioning goals, begin by consulting with your golf professional and tournament chairman. Schedule a planning session with them months in advance of the tournament, so that you have adequate time to involve your staff and start conditioning the golf course.

### NOTE

To achieve peak condition for the event, the turfgrass may be pushed to the limits; but if done properly, it will survive and continue to be healthy for the remainder of the prime golfing season. Put another way, the golf course can be peaked for special events and returned to normal conditioning without causing turf loss due to stressing during the tournament.

Tournament conditioning goals may be similar for each event that takes place on your course, or they may be totally different, depending on the type of course or club. If, say, you are conditioning for the club's member guest, you'll have to take into consideration that the majority of those playing will probably be higher-handicap players. Therefore, you may want to keep the rough cut lower than what it would be for the club championship, where the majority of players will carry a lower handicap. Likewise for the green speed: Whereas many club members may want the greens to roll at very quick speeds, you'll have to adjust the speed for higher-handicap players, who are not accustomed to fast greens; otherwise, the time it takes to play the round of golf will increase and may impede the participants' enjoyment of the tournament.

Your objective is twofold: to provide playing conditions appropriate to the situation—whether to challenge the best players at the club or accommodate higher-handicap guests—and to showcase the facility (and the work of you and your staff) to the players and the spectators.

*Working within a Budget*

In meeting tournament conditioning goals, you will inevitably be restricted by the maintenance budget that has been established for the year. This budget will, ideally, include a line item for "special tournaments" or "member-guest." Not only will this help you to set the appropriate conditioning goals, it also will make it easier to adjust your plans should the tournament committee members and/or tournament chairman change along the way, bringing with them new ideas. This line item should be treated as any other when determining the budget for the upcoming year, and anything that is to be done differently from the previous year should be addressed and the budget adjusted appropriately.

If the tournament line item in the budget is to be cut, make sure you find out what will be expected of you and your staff as preparations begin for a tournament. Obviously, it is neither practical nor reasonable for club management to decrease the budget and expect you to achieve the same conditions as in previous years.

With the budget set, you can more effectively explain why special conditioning goals may not be able to be met. For example, you can point out there is no money for the overtime required to hand-rake bunkers, and that they will have to be machine-raked as usual.

## AS THE TOURNAMENT DATE NEARS

Once you have completed all the necessary inventories (maintenance facility, equipment, golf course, and staffing), addressed any long-term agronomic problems, established the conditioning goals and the budget you'll need to meet them, you're on the home stretch. At the same time, the pressure will be mounting, so managing your time wisely, and that of everyone else involved, will be of the essence.

As the countdown begins, nothing will be more important than working closely with your team. Begin by scheduling a series of meetings with your planning team that will carry you all right up to the date of the tournament. These meetings should be well planned, short, and efficient—there's no time to waste now. If meeting on-site is difficult due to conflicting schedules of committee members, conference calls may be used. But as time nears for the tournament, I strongly recommend you arrange to have everyone meet on-site and in person.

Once again, you'll want work backward from the tournament date to set the dates and times for these meetings. For example, from three weeks to six weeks out, the meetings will be weekly. (Farther out than that, meetings can be every two weeks, three weeks, or monthly, depending on the amount of work that must be done and the number of people involved.) Instruct all members of the committee to come prepared with an explanation of what they are working on, what they need to complete their tasks on time, and from whom they need it. This ensures that no detail will be overlooked. Two weeks out from the tournament, the meeting agenda will be similar but the meetings may be every other day.

During these meetings, you and your team may realize it will be more productive to form one or more subcommittees to accomplish very specific tasks, such as locating the position of skyboxes, bleachers, and portable restrooms or setting up areas to be used for hospitality. These subcommittees can meet separately from the main committee, as needed to accomplish their assignments, but a representative from each should be charged with reporting back at the main tournament committee meetings.

Plan for the tournament to include such tasks as mowing frequencies and watering practices. (Details of tournament preparation practices are described later in this book.) Develop a rough draft of the plan and distribute it to your staff, requesting their input and suggested changes. Often, you'll find, the best ideas come from those "in the trenches," the staff members doing the daily work. Don't forget to set a firm date by which you want to receive their feedback.

Once you're confident you have covered all your bases, incorporate all necessary changes to the rough draft, to produce a final draft of your tournament plan. Distribute this to the committee, so there is no doubt in anyone's mind which maintenance practices will take place, and when. Do not, however, misinterpret the word "final" to mean inflexible. It's critical that you build into your plan a strategy for dealing with factors beyond your control, such as weather and, subsequently, changing course conditions. Ideally, you won't have to use that adjustment strategy, but be sure you have one. Detail in the plan what will be done if, for example, weather conditions leading up to and during the tournament will be wet; conversely, spell out how you plan to handle extremely dry or stressed turf conditions. You want the committee to be aware that if factors out of your control make it impossible to meet the ideal conditioning goals for the tournament, you and your staff will make every effort to come as close as possible without jeopardizing the golf course.

## CONDUCT A TRIAL RUN

With the final plan in place, it is time to make a trial run. This is an important tool for showing you and your staff where improvement is needed in your plan. (I think you will find that conducting trial runs will also help you improve everyday routine maintenance, as well.) Wait for conditions that will enable you to run a fair test, and coordinate with your staff to simulate as closely as possible all tournament-week events and activities, including when you work split shifts. Start conditioning the golf course as you will for the tournament: aim to increase your green speed; hand-rake bunkers if you will be doing so during the tournament; in short, do everything you have outlined in your plan for the event.

After the trial run is complete, sit down with your staff and evaluate the effectiveness of your plan. Look for ways to be more efficient, ways to reduce stress on the turf, ways to help you all do a better job during the actual tournament. Pay particular attention to the response of the greens as you start your tournament maintenance routine. Record the increase in green speed that you get with a double-cut versus a single-cut; note how much speed you pick up with a roll, and how much with the combination of a double-cut in the morning and single-cut and roll in the evening. Keep in mind that these speeds will only be approximations. For example, if you are doing your trial in the spring, and your tournament is in the summer, the greens may be wetter during the test, so the speeds you record will be a little off. The point of the test is to give you a general idea of what you will need to do to pick up six inches or a foot on a Stimpmeter (see Chapter Three for more on this tool). That way, as the tournament nears, you'll be better able to ascertain how to achieve your green speed conditioning goal.

Continue to fine-tune your maintenance practices right up to the tournament date. Take advantage of any outings you may have at your golf course just prior to the event. If, for example, a shot-gun start will be part of your tournament (e.g., for a Pro-Am), note how long it takes you to prepare the golf course prior to the start.

## SUMMARY

Nothing is more important to the success of any golf tournament, large or small, than a well-thought-out and implemented plan. Developing an effective plan is possible only when you collabo-rate with all those who will be involved with the tournament—the club's golf professional, tournament chairman, and, of course, your staff. When you solicit input, advice, and suggestions from these parties from the get-go, not only will you gain important information that will help you and your staff do your jobs better, but you will ensure that everyone takes a vested interest in carry-ing out the plan, which is just the kind of motivation you want to encourage.

Your final tournament plan may take many forms, depending on your golf organization and the people you work with. It can be as formal as a professionally produced and bound document or as simple as a hand-drawn timeline that is taped to a wall, with specific events highlighted. More often these days, it may be in electronic format, so that it can be widely and quickly distributed and accessed by tournament committee participants via com-puter. But whatever form it takes, make sure your final plan in-cludes all the inventories outlined in this chapter, as well as the strategies you and your team have decided to implement to make your event successful.

And, remember, build in flexibility so that as things change, your plan can change, too, with the minimum of disruption, to the club, management, the players, your staff and, of course, yourself.

With this overview in mind, it's time to get down to specifics. Here's the layout of the rest of the book:

• Chapter Two details how to implement an effective agronomic program.

- Chapter Three covers greens management.
- Chapter Four tells you all you need to know about preparing tees, fairways, and roughs for tournament play.
- Chapter Five is devoted to bunkers.
- Chapter Six delves into near-term tournament preparations and follow-up.
- The appendix provides pretournament checklists.

# CHAPTER TWO

# IMPLEMENTING AN EFFECTIVE AGRONOMIC PROGRAM

Too often, golf course superintendents find themselves battling poor turf conditions caused by failure to follow good basic agronomic principles. For example, they use less nitrogen than the plant requires in order to help with green speed, or they aerify only one time per season to prevent interruption of play (and member disgruntlement), or they topdress every four weeks instead of every two weeks to accommodate a busy course schedule.

That is why preparation for any tournament must start with a solid agronomic program. Using good, fundamental turfgrass science will allow you, the golf course superintendent, to push the golf course to extremes for short periods of time, while assuring a healthy recovery.

This program will include:

- Soil and tissue testing and soil amendments
- Proper fertilization
- Proper mowing practices
- Effective irrigation techniques
- Cultural control practices
- Timely pest management

# SOIL AND TISSUE TESTING AND SOIL AMENDMENTS

Soil testing is a primary contributor to a sound agronomic program. It will reveal the level of nutrients in the soil, as well as the amount of nutrients available to the turfgrass plant. This is an invaluable tool for evaluating nutrient levels and making recommendations on fertility programs. Soil testing can, in fact, be one of the most important processes that a golf course superintendent performs; for although there may be adequate nutrients in the soil, they may be tied up by chemical processes and so be unavailable to the plants. Soil testing will also alert you to potential salinity and toxicity issues.

Tissue testing, which measures the nutrients that have been taken up by the plant, is a relatively new concept now being used by golf course superintendents. It is a promising tool, and most reputable soil-testing laboratories can perform this service, but be aware it has not been perfected to the point at which it can be used alone to determine fertility recommendations. That is, at this time, it cannot replace soil testing.

The soil testing process can be done one of two ways: the golf course staff can collect the soil samples or a sampling company can be hired to do the entire process from collecting the samples and sending them to the lab to observing the lab results and making recommendations. If you choose to do the process in house, you should follow these steps:

- Select a reputable lab and obtain sampling bags and instructions on the lab's requirements so that the desired results will be obtainable.
- Decide what your sampling needs are such as greens, tees, fairways, and roughs (this may be determined by the condition of the turf in certain areas of the golf course or by the budget).
- If you have healthy turf conditions it may be wise to set your golf course up on a 3-year rotation where you are sampling 6 greens, 6 tees, and 6 fairways each year so that over the period of 3 years you have sampled the entire golf course.
- For greens and tees, take samples from a random cross section of each green and tee to be tested. It may be easiest to draw the

green on paper and diagram out your intended path of collection, usually a circle around the outer edges followed by an "X" shaped pattern through the center yields good results. Be sure to include any problem areas in separate bags so that particular needs of that area can be addressed.

- For fairways and roughs, you should follow a random pattern collecting from the outside edges of the fairway as well as the middle of the fairway. The rough should be a random sampling. Again if there are problem areas in a certain fairway be sure to sample those areas separately.

- Once all of the samples are collected (be sure to identify each bag as you are collecting the sample) they can be shipped to the testing lab.

- Be sure to keep all of the testing reports you receive so that comparisons can be made to ensure any treatments made to correct deficiencies are working.

Once you have completed your soil testing and have interpreted the results, you are ready to start correcting any deficiencies that might be present. Work very closely with your chemical and fertilizer supplier to ensure you are getting exactly what you need and that you understand at what rate to apply the material, so that no turf injury will occur. Keep in mind, many products are coated, and you need to know what is in that coating so that you do not exacerbate a problem (through the coating) you are trying to correct.

Throughout the process of correcting deficiencies, you will conduct soil testing to ensure you are getting the results you want. In most situations, soil testing should be done every 6 to 12 months, although in rare cases such as dealing with salt-affected turfgrass sites, extremely stressed turf, or very bad soil conditions, it may be necessary to test more often.

## PROPER FERTILIZATION

Proper fertilization is, of course, important not only for tournaments but for growing healthy turf in general. Every turfgrass plant has a recommended range of fertilization required during each growing season to keep it healthy. It is beyond the scope of this book to address the fertilization requirements for all turfgrass plants, so I recommend you consult one of the numerous books available on the subject such as Dr. James Beard's "Turf Management for Golf Courses," Dr. Nick Christian's "Fundamentals of Turfgrass Management," or Dr. A.J. Turgeon's "Turfgrass Management."

In terms of tournament preparation, your goal is to make sure each plant is healthy going into the stressful circumstances of the tournament. That will enable you to push the playing conditions to the limit without fear of turf loss during the tournament or after the event has concluded.

Opinions differ regarding the use of granular fertilizer versus liquid fertilizer. Some golf course superintendents like to use granular fertilizer during the spring and fall, and liquid during the summer. Others like to use granular only in the fall and liquid the rest of the growing season. To make this decision for your course, refer to the results of your soil tests (and tissue tests, if you conducted those, too). If the soil tests show adequate nutrition is available in the soil, using granular feeding only in the fall will suffice. If, on the other hand, the soil and tissue tests reveal certain nutrients are lacking, using granular in the spring and fall makes more sense. This is where tissue tests are particularly valuable, as they give you another important guideline for deciding when to use granular and when to "spoon-feed" liquid fertilizer.

## SPOON FEEDING

If you are one of those superintendents who opts to spoon-feed with liquids throughout the year, it's important to make sure you are calculating amounts properly so that the plants get enough nutrients to keep them healthy and growing. Your goal is to keep the plant growing, but not excessively. More on spoon-feeding in Chapter Three.

Which fertilizer you use and how much you use will also depend on timing. For example, as the tournament nears, you may want to increase the green speed, meaning you will want the plant to be a little leaner; or if your greens have too much speed, and

TABLE 2.1. TRACKING FERTILIZER APPLICATION IN RELATION TO GREEN SPEED

| Liquid Product | Amount N/1000 | Weeks to Event | Clipping Yield | Green Speed |
|---|---|---|---|---|
| 20-20-20 | 1/8 lb | 8 weeks | 1/8 basket | 9.5 feet |
| 18-3-3 | 2/10 lb | 7 weeks | 1/4 basket | 9 feet |
| 18-3-3 | 1/10 lb | 5 weeks | 1/4 basket | 9.5 feet |
| 20-20-20 | 1/8 lb | 3 weeks | 1/4 basket | 9.5 feet |
| 20-20-20 | 1/10 lb | 2 weeks | 1/4 basket | 10.5 feet |
|  | No Application | Tournament week | 1/8 basket | 10.5 feet |

you will need to slow them down, you will need some turf growth
to accomplish this (see Table 2.1). A good guideline for tournament preparation is to get approximately one-eighth to one-
quarter of a bucket of grass from mowing each morning (using a
typical walking-greens mower bucket). This amount tells you that
there is adequate but not excessive growth, and that you are in
control of the growth of the green. One practice you must avoid
is starving the turfgrass plant to achieve green speed. Certainly,
this will achieve higher green speed in the short term, but you
may find the long-term detriment to the plant to be too high a
price to pay for it.

Now comes the hard part: determining the amount of nitrogen in liquid form that will give you the growth you want during
the period leading up to the tournament. There are many different brands of liquid fertilizer on the market; the key is finding
one that works well for you at your golf course, and sticking with
it. Here's a good process to follow:

1. Begin using the fertilizer well in advance of your tournament
   and pay close attention to the amount of clippings you get
   the day after application.
2. Track the amount of clippings for the next few days until you
   see them start to fall off.
3. Change the rate of application the next time and make the
   same observations.

Eventually, you will find the rate and the frequency of application that works well on your golf course and gives you consistent,

controllable growth. Typically, one-tenth to one-eighth a pound of nitrogen every 10 to 14 days will give the desired results.

Once you have the product or products you want to use, you can determine when you will make your last application prior to the tournament start. As described in Chapter One, work backward from the start date of your tournament and to the day you want to make the application. Let's say that during your fertilizer trials you were getting 10 days of controlled growth from your product; that means you would want to make your last application so that the tenth day following it fell after the tournament concluded. Thus, if your tournament started on Thursday and ended on Sunday, you would want to make your last application the Friday before the start of the tournament. If the event is a two-day affair, say Saturday and Sunday, you could make the application anywhere from the Friday to the Wednesday prior to the event. Using this method to calculate when to make the last application will enable you to keep your greens healthy while allowing only the growth you desire to maintain green speed.

## BEWARE NEW-PRODUCT PROMISES

There are always new agronomic products coming on the market, and inevitably they promise fantastic results. As a golf course superintendent, you must overlook the marketing hoopla and find out what such products really do.

Start by asking the salesperson for scientific proof of the claims being made. If that proof is not available, and you are still interested in the product, set up your own trials and determine firsthand whether the claims are true. And even if results are promising, don't rely on the product(s) to the exclusion of basic agronomic practices. If you do, your turf will start to suffer.

# PROPER MOWING PRACTICES

To a golf course superintendent, proper mowing practices are critical on a regular basis, and more so when preparing for tournament play.

Proper mowing practices can be broken into six categories:

- Choosing the right mower for the job
- Cutting height
- Cutting frequency
- Mowing patterns
- Mower care
- Operator training

By addressing these six practices, you will be able to eliminate stress on the turfgrass plant, and thus improve your chances of achieving your conditioning goals for the tournament.

## Choosing the Right Mower for the Job

There are many great mowers on the market today, each capable of giving a precision cut in the height range it is manufactured for. The key, then, is to identify where the mower will be used and what its primary function will be. For example, if you have undulating greens, the floating-head greens mowers seem to provide the best cut at low heights as they travel over the contours; most important, at low cutting heights, these mowers tend to reduce or eliminate "scalping." If your golf course is located in a residential area, an electric mower may be ideal for your operation. Here are other mower features to consider when you are shopping for a new mower:

- *Bed bar*: Discuss the cutting height you will be using with the manufacturer, because at today's lower mowing heights, the thickness of the bed bar becomes very important. Most manufacturers make a thinner bed bar, but it is not standard equipment on a new purchase. If this is the bed bar you need to achieve the desired cutting height, you will want to negotiate this as part of your purchase agreement.
- *Mower width*: Greens mowers come in varying widths. There are the "tournament stripe," or 18-inch, and the standard 22-inch. Some manufacturers also offer walking greens mowers in 26-inch width, but these are used primarily for tees or approaches. And most manufacturers make a quality triplex mower for those who triplex-cut their greens.

- *Ease of operation*: In consideration of your staff, you will want to evaluate the mower for ease of operation and comfort of control features.

### Mower Options

An important question to ask the manufacturer is what mower options are available. These may include:

- Rollers
- Verticut heads
- Groomer attachments
- Backlap options
- Eleven-blade reels

When it comes to cutting tees and fairways, typically there are many options to choose from. For tees, some clubs hand-mow while others triplex-cut. If you are hand-mowing tees, 26-inch cut mowers are available. If you choose to triplex-cut your tees, the same mowers used for greens will work well for tees. Two things to consider carefully are height of cut and type of grass on your tees. These two factors will determine the number of blades you will need on your reels for the tee mowers. The lower the height of cut, and the thinner the leaf blade on the grass you are cutting, the more blades you want. There are many different types of mower blades available, and you will want to include one that meets your needs. For example:

- For low-cut bentgrass or Bermuda grass tees (3/8-inch), you will want 11-blade reels.
- For higher-cut bentgrass, bluegrass, and the like (7/16-inch, 1/2-inch, and higher) eight-blade reels will work well.

The typical choices for fairway mowers are the triplex or the fiveplex. Again, all manufacturers offer quality machines, so it will be up to you to know the number of blades you will need on your reels and the weight of the head—lightweight greens mower heads or heavier fairway heads. Here, too, the determining factors will be your conditioning goals and the type of turf you have on your fairways. Fine-cut turf can be achieved using the lightweight heads; but if you have turf that is prone to producing thatch, you will need an aerification and topdressing program to control it. If you are limited by budget or time for aerification, or if your turf is thicker, coarser, or higher cut, you may opt to use a heavier cutting head. Your particular situation will dictate your choice in cutting heads.

When it comes to surrounds mowers, you must look at the terrain that makes up the green, tee, and fairway surrounds. There are a number of reel mowers on the market that give an excellent-quality cut in these areas while making quick work of the job. The reel mowers are also resistant to scalping, in most cases. The rotary mowers on the market also give a good quality of cut and make the mowing job very efficient; however, if there are undulations in the surround areas you are cutting, and the desired height of cut is down around 1 inch, if the rotary being considered will cut that low, you may experience some scalping in the undulated areas. If your surrounds are relatively flat, a rotary mower may be an excellent choice.

For roughs, some course superintendents are still using reel mowers, but most have switched to rotary mowers. Today's rotary mowers give a great quality cut while standing the turf up. They are available in many different widths and can make quick work of cutting the roughs. There are also antiscalp devices available from most manufacturers, which enable the mowers to travel over undulating terrain without leaving a mark. The turn radius on most of these units also lets an experienced operator trim around trees and other items as they travel around the course. For areas around the clubhouse, the zero-turn rotary mowers can be very handy.

Because many of today's mowers are so close in quality, a number of other factors will come into play in choosing the right mower:

- *The local distributor*: A good relationship with the distributor is vital. For example, will the distributor offer loaner equipment when your mower is in the repair shop for service, or if you need additional equipment for special events?
- *Post-sales service*: The service arrangement is as important, if not more so, than the sale itself.

- *Availability of parts*: You don't want to have to wait days or weeks to get a part replaced, especially with a tournament just around the corner.

## PROPER CUTTING HEIGHT

Every turfgrass species has a recommended cutting height range (see Table 2.2), and it is incumbent upon golf course superintendents to remember what that range is for the turfgrass grown on their courses. What superintendent hasn't gotten into trouble when trying to gain green speed, or make fairway turf perform a certain way, and ended up stressing the turf because the cutting height was too low? Case in point is the daily-fee golf course, where superintendents are often forced to cut the rough lower than the preferred height so that golfers can easily find their golf balls.

TABLE 2.2. SUGGESTED CUTTING HEIGHTS FOR COMMON TURFGRASS SPECIES

| Turfgrass Species | Cutting Height Range (in.) |
| --- | --- |
| Colonial bentgrass | 0.0–1.0 |
| Creeping bentgrass | 0.1–0.7 |
| Velvet bentgrass | 0.2–0.6 |
| Annual bluegrass | 0.2–1.0 |
| Kentucky bluegrass | 1.0–2.5 |
| Rough bluegrass | 0.5–1.5 |
| Fine fescues | 0.5–2.0 |
| Tall fescue | 1.75–3.0 |
| Perennial ryegrass | 1.5–2.0 |
| Bahia grass | 1.5–3.0 |
| Bermuda grass common | 0.6–1.5 |
| Bermuda grass hybrid | 0.1–0.5 |
| Carpet grass | 1.0–3.0 |
| Centipede grass | 1.0–3.0 |
| Buffalo grass | 0.5–unmowed |
| Kikuyu grass | 0.7–2.0 |
| Seashore paspalum | 0.5–2.0 |
| St. Augustine grass | 1.5–4.0 |
| Zoysia grass | 0.5–2.0 |

Superintendents need to communicate proper cutting heights to their boards and owners, and back up this information with documentation. If certain cutting heights are desired by the players of the club, it may well be worth the investment in regrassing (greens, tees, and fairways) and using a turfgrass variety that is better suited to the desired cutting height. There are numerous turfgrass varieties on the market today that will withstand today's lower cutting heights.

Never lose sight of the basic effects of cutting height on the turfgrass plant. That is, lower cutting heights tend to decrease carbohydrates, leaf width, root growth, and rhizome growth; conversely, they increase shoot density, succulence of the shoot tissues, and stress.

## PROPER CUTTING FREQUENCY

Proper cutting frequency is related directly to cutting height—the lower the cutting height, the more frequent the turf must be cut. More specifically, follow the one-third rule: Do not remove more than one-third of the leaf blade in any one cutting. Greens that are typically kept at heights of 0.125 inch to 0.156 inch are cut everyday, whereas roughs that are typically cut at 2 inches or higher are cut once or twice per week, depending on the growing conditions.

Remember, too, that in times of turf stress, it is appropriate to raise the height of cut and decrease the frequency thereby alleviating stress.

## PROPER MOWING PATTERNS

Mowing patterns are extremely important on the golf course, and they vary according to the individual golf course superintendent; however, the outcome is usually the same. Most superintendents mow greens in four different directions: east, west, north, and south; or with the fairway, across, left to right and right to left.

On tees and fairways, the patterns can be similar or be reduced to two directions and repeated with alternate patterns from time to time to help alleviate the grainy condition caused by mowing the same pattern repeatedly. Another way to help reduce the incidence of grain is to vary the mowing direction each time you mow. Many superintendents use 45-degree angles (left to right and right to left) or straightaway striping. Other patterns are becoming more popular as well, such as half-and-half mowing and one-way mowing. (Note: Tee and fairway mowing patterns are discussed in greater detail later in the book.)

Brushing is another technique that will aid with grain control. Brushing the greens in different directions over the course of a few days, and mowing after or during the brushing, will stand the grass blades up and allow for a much cleaner cut and less grain.

Collars, step-cuts, and roughs are usually cut in one direction and then mown in the opposite direction the next time they are cut. Some golf course superintendents have started using rotary mowers that stripe in the roughs, and incorporating patterns in these areas. They are also changing cutting patterns, similar to the practice on the fairways.

## PROPER MOWER CARE

The importance of care and maintenance of your mowing equipment cannot be overstated. Dull blades and reels tear the leaf blade and give the turf a whitish appearance, and leave behind an open wound that attracts disease and insects. Worn roller bearings result in the mower cutting lower on one side—possibly even scalping the turf, leading to severe injury and uneven putting conditions on the putting surface. By properly sharpening the reels and blades and greasing the bearings regularly, you will ensure clean-cut turf mowed at the correct height.

If you use mowers that are hydraulically driven, make sure their hydraulic hoses are inspected routinely to prevent hydraulic leaks on finely cut turf areas, which almost always lead to dead turf. Areas on putting greens where leaks have occurred may take weeks to heal before they are again suitable as hole locations. On fairways and tees, these areas can be sodded, but may be unplayable until the sod "roots in." Damaged fairway areas will need to be marked as "ground under repair"; and on the teeing surface, the area will need to be kept off-limits for a prolonged period of time.

A good mechanic will institute a daily routine that will ensure the mowing equipment is ready for use the next time it is needed. This routine will include:

- Backlapping and adjusting reels prior to each mowing
- Checking hydraulic hoses weekly
- Checking oil levels on a daily basis
- Grinding blades and reels as necessary
- Checking tire pressure
- Facing bedknives as necessary
- Ensuring bearings are properly greased by the operators; greasing those areas the operators cannot get to on a daily basis
- Checking the cutting height prior to each mowing
- Checking the water/coolant level, or making sure airways are clear on air-cooled engines, on a regular basis
- Checking for fuel leaks every day

It's a good idea to put these tasks on a checklist to make sure they are done consistently, to ensure that the equipment is operating correctly at all times and producing the quality of the cut you and the players are expecting.

## PROPER OPERATOR TRAINING

The best mower in the world won't do the job it's intended for if the person operating it hasn't been trained correctly. This training, which should begin the first day an employee is on the job, can be carried out in a classroom setting, in the maintenance building, or club house, and be reinforced in the field. It is also through the training process that you, as superintendent, relate the expectations of the golf course patrons and emphasize the importance of proper equipment maintenance.

When it comes to mowing, explain to the operators:

- Why straight lines and smooth cuts are important
- What happens when a mower has a hydraulic leak and it goes unseen for an extended period of time
- What effect missed areas on a green will have on ball roll
- What concerns to raise when a mower is leaving streaks on a green, tee, or fairway

- How to spot a hydraulic leak
- What a streak caused by a mower looks like
- What to do when the cut is not correct

In sum, a properly trained operator should know what to do when things are not right in every circumstance. Never pass up the opportunity to use problems as a teaching tool—for example, show operators streaks caused by mowers, hydraulic leaks, and scalp injury. This will help them know what to look for and to make the correct response, immediately.

Finally, both you and the equipment mechanic should spend time with new operators to explain what constitutes normal performance on the mowers they will be using.

## EFFECTIVE IRRIGATION TECHNIQUES

Water management is critical to growing healthy turf. When it comes to making tournament play a successful experience, the best surface is a firm, fast surface. This is accomplished by being very judicious with water. Once the turf is in the condition you want, the key is to add only the amount of water needed to make the turf survive until the next water cycle. And for turf to survive when conditions change or turn out other than what is forecast, hand-watering will become part of a successful water management strategy. (These techniques will be discussed in depth later in the book when I discuss management of the various golf course areas.)

## CULTURAL CONTROL PRACTICES

A major component in managing healthy turfgrass is using good cultural control practices. I've covered a number of those already—mowing height and frequency, irrigation, and fertilization. This section addresses six more:

- Aerification
- Topdressing
- Spiking
- Verticutting

- Grooming
- Brushing

Each of these practices plays a major role in growing healthy turf, and must be done at the proper time; no one can replace another.

## AERIFICATION

Tees, fairways, and even roughs should be aerified on a regular basis. High-traffic areas around cart paths can be vastly improved by aeration two to four times per year. And for tournament preparation, don't forget to aerify areas around the clubhouse, as this will be the first impression of the facility that the golfer receives.

There are many ways to aerify:

- Hollow-tine (also called hollow-core)
- Solid-tine
- Deep-tine
- Water injection
- Dry injection

Each of these has its place, but the most essential is hollow-tine aerification, where a core of soil is pulled out and left on the surface.

- Hollow-tine aerification should be done two to four times per year on greens, depending on the condition of the soil and amount of play and stress on the golf course.
- Solid-tine aeration with small tines (usually 1/4 to 1/8 inch) is an effective way to open up space in which water and air can travel during the stress of summer weather, but it should not be used to replace hollow-tine aeration.
- Deep-tine aeration allows penetration down through the soil profile, 11 to 12 inches deep, to help alleviate layers that may form from aerifying to the same depth year after year. This practice should be used to complement hollow-tine aeration.
- Water injection and dry injection are two other ways to aerify in the summer months, to open up air and water space without

major disruption to the surface. Here too, these methods do not replace hollow-tine aeration.

Spiking is another way to open up shallow air pockets that will allow for water penetration when the soil is in need of oxygen and moisture; when more disruptive operations such as hollow-tine aeration cannot be performed.

## TOPDRESSING

Topdressing, the practice of smoothing the putting surface while helping to maintain a healthy soil profile, is one of the most important cultural practices superintendents perform. When aerifying, it is important to apply enough topdressing material so that all of the holes are filled completely, but not so much that there is excess sand on the surface, which must be removed by hand.

Currently, superintendents are topdressing lightly and more frequently, applying material weekly or every two weeks, depending on soil conditions and the amount of play the golf course receives. Light applications (merely a dusting) work very well for keeping thatch in check and maintaining a smooth putting surface. It is important that the topdressing program keep up with the growth of the turf and thatch production. This will expedite growing healthy turf and, occasionally, speeding up the greens for special occasions by allowing smoother ball roll.

On tees, similar practices should be implemented, making sure the topdressing program keeps pace with the growth of the turf. Although there are still many golf courses with native-soil tees, a more recent trend on newly constructed courses is to build the tee surfaces out of the same material used on the putting greens. Fairway topdressing is becoming common practice at golf courses that can afford the extra expense. Undoubtedly, this will make the fairways perform better as the soil profile becomes modified, but the practice is very costly.

## VERTICUTTING

Done in conjunction with aerifying and topdressing, verticutting plays a vital role in maintaining a healthy soil profile. Since the introduction of groomers, however, many golf course superintendents have set verticutters on the shelf and replaced them with groomers. But these are two very different functions:

- Groomers are used to help keep grain in check by vertically mowing the top part of the turf and helping the grass blade to grow in a more upright position. Groomers are typically spaced very close together.
- Verticutters can be used to groom by setting the depth very shallow so that it just "tickles" the top of the turf. Verticutters are also used to do vertical mowing, whereby thatch is removed from the soil profile. Verticut blades can be spaced quite close or adjusted farther apart if there is extreme thatch and then moved closer together for routine verticutting once the thatch is under control.

Verticutting and grooming give the maximum benefit when they can be performed over multiple days and in different directions, preferably at 90-degree angles and in four different directions, as discussed earlier in the section on mowing.

An important point to remember about all cultural practices is that they are effective methods for improving or maintaining turf health, *when done at the proper time.* But they also cause stress to the turf, and that is why it is just as important to know when *not* to carry out these practices. The last thing you want is to push the turfgrass plant over the edge just prior to your most important tournament of the year.

## TIMELY PEST MANAGEMENT

Turfgrass pests come in two primary types: ones such as insects and disease, use the plant as a host, feeding upon it or using its nutrients to grow larger and stronger; the second type, such as weeds, compete with the turfgrass plant for nutrients, water, and space in which to grow. Successful pest management involves knowing which pests are present, and where on the golf course, and when is the proper time to apply pesticides.

As superintendent, you will lay out a plan to address every pest present on your golf course. For starters, you'll need to familiarize yourself with the products available and relevant in your location. In the United States, the availability of products and use restrictions can vary widely from state to state. Contact your state regulatory department that oversees agricultural chemicals for specifics where you are.

Your plan should also spell out when to look for each pest and when to institute control measures. By being attentive in this matter, you will also find opportunities to reduce chemical applications. For example, you'll be able to select pesticides that take care of multiple pests, or mix chemicals that will take care of different pests while minimizing the number of applications that must be made, thus saving on labor and wear and tear on the golf course.

An important part of your plan will be to make sure that staff applying the pesticides read and understand the pesticide label, prior to using them. Application timing, is, of course, important, and that will be discussed in greater detail in later chapters as it relates to each area of the golf course.

## SUMMARY

Simply put, you cannot prepare a golf course successfully for a tournament without sound agronomic principles in place. The fertilization program must be balanced and in line with the needs and requirements of the turf species, as determined by soil and tissue testing. Mowing practices must be within the limits of the variety of turfgrass chosen for the particular area of the golf course. Choosing the proper mowing equipment, and ensuring that it is properly maintained and ready for the job at hand, will ensure the proper cut, alleviate stress, and minimize entry points for disease and insects.

Good irrigation practices will ensure that the plant is getting adequate moisture, without being overwatered. A guideline is to give the plant only what it will need to survive until the next irrigation cycle, and supplement with hand-watering, as necessary. Combining good water management with cultural practices will help the water penetrate through a minimal thatch layer and be available for take-up by the turfgrass roots.

Finally, to keep the turf areas on the golf course in top condition, you and your staff must constantly scout the course for turfgrass pests, and be aware of weather and other environmental factors that influence those pests. High-quality turfgrass can be maintained with timely pesticide applications, at minimal rates.

Chapter Three, "Greens Management," will build on the information in this chapter, to help move the golf course closer to ideal tournament conditions.

# GREENS MANAGEMENT

Establishing a comprehensive and efficient agronomics program frees you up to start focusing on preparing the golf course for the actual event. You will need to start many of the activities and tasks involved in this preparation months ahead of the actual tournament date, to give you time to condition the golf course so that it will be strong enough to withstand the stress of the event activities. Think of this process as analogous to the training marathon runners undergo when preparing for a race, so that when the time comes, they can push themselves to the limit yet recover in short order. You are aiming for the same type of response from your golf course. Healthy turf that is growing properly can be cut, rolled, topdressed, and played upon by hundreds of players for multiple days then recover in a very short time frame.

In Chapter One I mentioned greens evaluation as part of the golf course inventory you conduct. In this chapter, I'll delve into the details of what to look for while surveying your greens. To begin, I'll cover:

- Contour and slope severity
- Adequate size
- Right grass for the job
- Good surface density and minimal grain
- Shade issues/problems

By inspecting each of these areas carefully, you'll know well in advance what improvements need to be made to each area to ready your golf course greens for your golf tournament.

# Contour and Slope Severity

Contour and slope severity are the two primary factors in determining speed of the greens and the type of mower that is best to use on the putting surface.

## Speed

Simply stated, the more contours a putting green has and the more severe the slopes, the slower the greens will need to be if you and your staff are to provide ideal hole locations for tournament play. Unfortunately, all too often greens speed for tournaments, whether for member-guests or club championships, are handed down to the golf course superintendent more or less in the form of edicts, by boards and committees, whose members frequently do not take into account the contours and slope on the course; the result is that certain hole locations become impossible to include on the tournament course.

The rule of thumb is that the golfer should be able to stop a properly struck putt within 3 feet of the hole coming down a slope or putting over a contour in the green. As briefly mentioned in Chapter One, you can use a Stimpmeter to measure greens speed and, subsequently, to ensure consistent greens speed for tournament play. (For more on the Stimpmeter, refer to the accompanying sidebar.)

---

## HISTORY AND USE OF THE STIMPMETER

The Stimpmeter, invented by Edward Stimson over 60 years ago, was designed to measure the speed of golf greens for the purpose of ensuring a consistent speed across the course. The intent is to find a speed the players are happy with, then use the stimpmeter to duplicate that speed on all the greens on the golf course. (Note: There is now another speed-measuring device on the market, called the Peltz Meter, developed by Dave Peltz.) This is still the ideal use of the Stimpmeter today, although many clubs now use greens speed as a status symbol and thus compare their

*(Continued)*

stimpmeter readings against the speed readings of other golf courses. In fact, some superintendents are required to post stimpmeter readings in various parts of the clubhouse.

In preparation for and during tournament, it is a good idea to take and record daily stimpmeter readings. For professional events, the daily speed will be posted in the rules officials' trailers. For local tournaments, such as member-guests, club championships, state and local tournaments, the information can be posted in the maintenance facility. In these cases, the readings are more of a tool for the golf course superintendent, to ensure that the greens speed is meeting the goals of the tournament.

To "stimp" a green, do the following:

- Find the most level area on the green to take the reading. (Note that the stimpmeter can also serve as a level, by laying it flat on

FIGURE 3.1. A STIMPMETER (U.S. VERSION, 36 INCHES LONG; U.K. VERSION, 1 METER) IS USED TO MEASURE GREENS SPEED AND, MORE IMPORTANTLY, ACHIEVE SPEED CONSISTENCY FROM GREEN TO GREEN.

the putting surface and placing the ball in the middle of the meter and watching for movement.)

- Always take the reading from the same point on the green.
- Identify which greens are to be stimped for tournament play. It is not necessary to stimp every green every day. Simply identify five to six greens that represent the other greens on the golf course and check the speed on those. Be sure to include the putting green, a green at the highest and lowest points of the golf course, one that is in the open and one that is in a wooded setting, and any green whose characteristics make the speed on it different from the others.
- Follow the instructions in the "USGA Stimpmeter Instruction Booklet" that comes with every stimpmeter purchased from the USGA.
- Make sure you use a level area on the green.
- Roll three golf balls in one direction and measure the distance.
- Roll the golf balls in the opposite direction and measure the distance.
- Take the average of the above two rolls and that will be the green speed for that green.
- If you take readings for multiple days, make sure you use the same locations—these locations can be marked by pushing a golf pencil into the green and filling the hole with white sand.

## Mowers

If your greens are marked by severe slopes and contours, chances are you will need mowers with floating heads, in order to prevent scalping as the mower moves over the edge of the slope. This type of mower has rollers that are closer together, allowing them to traverse the slope without gouging or scalping the turf at the crest of the slope.

As part of your greens preparation, contact mower manufacturers and ask for a demonstration of their floating-head mowers, until you find the one that enables you to mow your greens without causing damage.

Just be aware that even with a good greens mower, you still may have to take additional preparatory steps to ease the severity of the slopes. For example, you may want to aerify along the top of the slope, over the slope, and just below the slope. Then, with those aerification holes open, roll the slopes with a greens roller or a water-injecting aerifier (with the water turned off). Afterward, try mowing with the floating-head greens mowers again, and see if you have corrected the problem.

## GREENS WITHOUT DRAINAGE

Greens built prior to the common practice of installing drainage (modern USGA type, etc.), usually "push-up greens," relied on the slope to carry water away (surface drainage) from the putting surface. Typically, these greens were also constructed at a time when green speeds were much slower. If you are faced with maintaining today's green speeds on this type of contoured greens, it's probably time to raise the question about rebuilding the greens with club management. If the decision is made to rebuild the greens, consult a golf course architect to make sure the job is done right. In many situations, the original features can be saved while softening the contours and adding internal drainage so that the green keeps some of its original characteristics yet becomes more highly functional in today's world of fast greens.

## ADEQUATE SIZE

If you have greens of adequate size, your life as a golf course superintendent will be a lot easier. With a good-size green, you can, for example, move a given hole location frequently enough so that the previous day's wear pattern rarely interferes with the current day's hole location. This will pay huge dividends when the green is under stress.

In general, greens that are 5,000 square feet or larger are considered adequate size; that said, the square footage of the green must, of course, be sized according to the amount of play the golf course receives. Obviously, the more play on a day-to-day basis, the larger the greens need to be.

## VARYING TRAFFIC PATTERNS

When approaching the challenge of varying traffic patterns, be sure to pay special attention to any practice putting greens and chipping greens, as they may receive much more traffic than those on the golf course. This harkens back to the issue of size. If you are one of those superintendents who must cope with heavy play on greens that are very small, and you cannot vary traffic patterns, it will be almost impossible to avoid the development of wear patterns, which means the turf will inevitably become stressed, ultimately resulting in turf loss. This loss can be minimized or avoided by using sound agronomic principals discussed in Chapter Two.

As the golf course superintendent, it is your responsibility to assess each green and make a determination as to its size in conjunction with the amount of rounds it receives; from that assessment, you'll determine whether any reconstruction needs to be done. If so, your first step should be to consult a golf course architect, then set up a meeting between you, the architect, and your superiors. The agenda for this meeting should be to determine the long-term best interest of the golf course. Based on that decision, the planning process will evolve for resolving the issue.

# TYPE OF GRASS

What type of grass is on the putting surfaces at your course? How has it has performed over the past few seasons? Have there been issues year after year with certain greens, or even all the greens?

These are the kinds of questions you, as course superintendent, need to ask yourself in regard to the type and variety of grass planted on the putting surfaces. If there are or have been issues, it's time to research some of the new varieties of grass that are available to determine whether there is a better type for your course. But do this only after you have exhausted all of the proper agronomic procedures. What you don't want to do is put a different variety or species of grass into the same bad agronomic conditions; that's just setting the new grass variety or species up to fail—and yourself, as well.

If, on the other hand, you determine there is a better grass for your course, do your homework on that product before bringing your conclusions to the decision makers. Be fully prepared to explain the benefits of regrassing the greens with this different variety/species of grass. (Note: This would also be an excellent time to address any drainage problems that might also exist on the greens. Here, too, explore this venture in depth before presenting it, as it can be a very costly undertaking.)

Regrassing is a task more easily done at a private club, where the membership can be informed and notified well in advance. In contrast, at a public course or daily-fee course, even one with good communication policies in place, it is difficult to make the playing public understand the eventual benefit of regrassing; it is also difficult to convince an owner to give up revenue for the time it takes to regrass the greens and grow them in to the point at which they are ready for play.

## Surface Density and Minimal Grain

Healthy turf grass will have good surface density. That means, as you look down into the turf canopy, you will not be able to see soil. Good surface density will also have a canopy that will accept top-dressing, leading to a very smooth surface. Adequate surface density will also help protect the green from pests, especially weed invasion. Along with ensuring good surface density and proper top-dressing, another related objective is to keep the amount of grain to a minimum. (You cannot totally eliminate the grain.) To check your greens for grain level, take a stiff-bristled broom out on a green and push the broom out as you turn around in a circle. This will let you see how much grain you have. Recall from Chapter Two on mowing patterns, and how mowing in four different directions was important for reducing grain. Another mowing pattern that will help reduce grain—and one that can be done in the weeks leading up to the tournament—is what is known as a "back cut," or "back-track" mowing. This is simply mowing a stripe in one direction and turning around and mowing the same stripe back in the opposite direction. It is a different type of double-cutting. When you do this as part of the normal maintenance practices, it will help reduce grain and allow a very true ball roll.

# SHADE ISSUES

It is the rare golf course that doesn't have one or two greens with shade issues, and some have many more. As the course superintendent, you are no doubt quite familiar where these locations are at your facility. But if not, say, you are new to your job, the best way to familiarize yourself with shady spots along the greens is to travel the course at different times of the day—especially during the mornings. Take along your camera on these surveys, to document these locations; be sure to note the time of day each picture was taken (see Figure 3.2). It's also a good idea to flag these areas, to more exactly show the extent of the shade at various times.

This documentation is critical to have on hand when addressing this problem with management at your course/club, for too often decision makers see the green when the sun is shining on it and don't realize how many hours a day it spends under shade. To supplement your own record keeping, avail yourself of

FIGURE 3.2. SHADE CAN CAUSE THE TURFGRASS ON PUTTING GREENS TO THIN OUT AND BE EXTREMELY DIFFICULT TO GROW. THE GOAL IS TO STRIKE A FINE BALANCE BETWEEN THOSE TREES THAT ARE NEEDED AND THOSE CAUSING PROBLEMS.

materials available from the *USGA Greens Section Record* and *Golf Course Management Magazine* that describe what shade does to turfgrass.

In terms of determining solutions to problems caused by shade, take a look at the green setting with an eye to removing some (or all) of the trees or other growth causing the shade issues, without drastically changing the look or playability of the setting. You might also want to solicit the services of one of the companies that can evaluate shade issues on putting greens using computer technology to measure precisely the amount and duration of light the green is receiving. This technology is so precise it can tell you which branches to remove from certain trees to improve the sunlight penetration to the green. Consulting one of these firms is a particularly good idea if the subject of trees, and their removal or thinning, is a sensitive one at your golf course. With objective advice and information to present, it is often easier to recommend solutions to the decision makers at your facility.

# GREENS MANAGEMENT TECHNIQUES

This section digs deeper into greens management, specifically addressing the health of the turfgrass on your course, to help you develop the tools and processes essential to producing top-quality, tournament-ready putting greens. The topics are:

* Root zone health
* Aerification
* Topdressing
* Fertilizer and pesticide programs
* Water management

## ROOT ZONE HEALTH

It's common knowledge among golf course superintendents that as the root zone goes, so goes the turf canopy. Therefore, it's imperative to examine the root zone frequently throughout the year, following these guidelines (Figure 3.3):

FIGURE 3.3. EXAMINE THE GREEN SOIL PROFILE MANY TIMES THROUGHOUT THE GROWING SEASON.

- Look at the thatch layer, paying close attention to how the top-dressing program is keeping up with the growth of the turf.
- Watch for layering, an indication that the topdressing program is not keeping up with the turf growth. Layering can cause drainage problems, which can lead to black layer, which can ultimately result in thinning or dying turf.
- Periodically check the root depth of the turfgrass plants, especially coming out of the winter months and going into the summer stress period. Take advantage of the fall and spring growing seasons to push the roots as deep as possible, so that the plant will be healthy going into winter and, subsequently, will be ready for the stresses of the summer season. A good healthy root system will also aid in recovery from stressful conditions as the summer comes to a close.
- Pay close attention to the percolation (perc) rate. If the golf green was built to USGA specifications, the sand used had a

percolation rate. Compare the present percolation rate against the original one. If it has slowed significantly, find a way to improve it. Core aerification followed by topdressing is one possibility; but more likely, if the percolation rate has slowed markedly, deep-tine aerification followed by topdressing will be necessary. And be aware that it may take several years of the corrective process to improve the percolation rate.

## AERIFICATION

I've mentioned several times that good aerification practices are a must when preparing a golf course for competition—especially today, with the trend to push turfgrass to the limits of its performance capabilities. As the golf course superintendent, you must educate the management team at your facility, as well as the members and players, about the benefits of aerification, including the ideal time for the process to occur. Unfortunately from the players' and members' point of view, this is usually when the greens are looking and playing their best. But they must be made to understand that aerifying at the proper time will allow the greens to heal as quickly as possible; when delayed—for example, to the approach of winter—plant growth starts to slow, making the healing time proportionately longer. Superintendents of daily-fee courses usually face the additional challenge of choosing between aerifying during good weather, which are also good revenue days, and delaying the process until such time as conditions are less conducive to playing golf, but also to plant recovery.

In northern climates especially, aerifying too late into the season causes superintendents to run the risk that holes won't heal before bad weather sets in; and if the winter happens to be cold, dry, and windy, the greens may suffer further from winter desiccation.

### Aerification Frequency and Timing Practices

How often you aerify will depend primarily on two factors: where your golf course is located and how much play it receives. The simple equation is, the longer the growing season and the more play, the more times per year the golf course will need to be aerified. That is not to say that a golf course that receives little play does not need to be aerified. Far from it. Aerification and topdressing (discussed in the next section) are two of the best ways to control thatch and maintain a healthy root zone on a course of any size and in any location.

When it comes to greens aerification, hollow-tining is extremely important; but here, too, it is incumbent upon you, as golf course superintendent, to evaluate the soil structure and decide if more is required on your course. Perhaps, for example, deep-tining may be necessary. Many golf course superintendents have found that deep-tine aerification, in addition to hollow-core aerification, produces a product that is much healthier under stressful situations (see Figures 3.4 and 3.5). Those superintendents who are trying to modify their root zone from native soil or a poor root zone mix may find it advantageous to deep-tine and topdress heavily, or use the drill-and-fill method to speed the conversion process.

FIGURE 3.4. HOLLOW-TINE AERIFICATION IS EXTREMELY IMPORTANT IN MAINTAINING HEALTHY TURFGRASS.

FIGURE 3.5. PERFORM DEEP-TINE AERIFICATION AS AN ADJUNCT TO THE HOLLOW-TINE PRACTICE—THE FORMER DOES NOT REPLACE THE LATTER.

## TOPDRESSING

Topdressing is defined generally as the act of applying material to land or a road without working it in. Whether this definition holds true, however, will depend on what you are trying to accomplish on your golf course. For example, if you are topdressing after aerification, it is advisable to apply enough topdress material to completely fill the holes, which would necessitate working it into the turf mat and the soil profile. If, on the other hand, you are applying the topdress material as part of the routine program of light and frequent topdressing, use just enough material so that it will not need to be worked in, but instead can be watered in, rolled in, or blown in using back-pack blowers set on low to medium idle.

### Choosing a Topdress Material

When picking a sand to use as a topdress material, I recommend you refer to the original specifications for the sand used during

greens construction and pick a product with comparable specifications. If this information is not available, send a small sample of
your current greens mix to a reputable soil-testing laboratory and
get it evaluated, so that you have a reference to guide you. Then,
when selecting a supplier for the topdress material, present the
specifications and ask to have them matched.

The preceding guideline is, however, relevant only if you are
satisfied with the results you have been getting. If your current
mix is *not* producing the results you want, take your current
greens mix specifications to a reputable USGA-approved testing
laboratory and ask for help in finding a sand mix that will help
improve the soil profile without causing a layering effect

In terms of sand types, remember that sand being dragged
over the leaf tissue causes stress on the turf plant. Sand that is
rounded will cause less injury than sand that has sharp angles
(which may cause abrasions, or actually cut the leaf tissue, leaving open wounds). The downside to round sand is that it has a
tendency to remain loose in the soil profile; conversely, the
upside to angled sand is that it will help the greens to become
firmer.

### Topdressing Application Program
With the proper sand selected you can implement your topdressing program. Follow these guidelines:

- As stated previously, when aerifying, apply enough sand to
  ensure all of the holes are filled in.
- Avoid applying excessive amounts of sand, which will cause un-
  due stress on the turfgrass plant, because of the extra dragging
  that will be needed to work in the additional material.
- Your normal program should consist of light, frequent topdressing throughout the growing season. The amount of
  material and the frequency will be directly proportionate to
  the amount of growth of the turfgrass plant.
- To ensure that your program is keeping up with growth, take a
  soil profile sample about once every four to six weeks and look
  for layering of materials. If you are seeing layering, it's a sign
  you will need to increase topdressing frequency. The profile
  should look like one continuous sand stratum.

*Types of Drags*

There are many types of drags available for working in the top-dress material—steel drag mats, different types of brooms and brushes, and fibrous mats. Each type has its place; at the same time, each type will impose some degree of stress on the turf.

- Steel mats tend to cause the most stress on the turf—although if used extensively, brooms and brushes can cause just as much stress.
- Fibrous mats, such as cocoa mats, seem to be the least stressful because of the softness of their material.
- Using brooms, and hand-brushing, is another low-stress method of topdressing. Unfortunately, this incurs a high cost of manpower.
- Blowers are another option for working the topdress material into the putting green surface. Using a back-pack blower or Buffalo blower, with the power turned down to the low position, is a good way to work in the material without a lot of stress on the turfgrass plant.

At all times, remember that topdressing, as necessary as it is, does put some stress on the turfgrass plant, so be sure to evaluate current climate conditions and the health of the turfgrass plants before deciding to apply the topdress material you have chosen.

## FERTILIZER AND PESTICIDE PROGRAMS

As a golf course superintendent, you will develop your own fertilizer and pesticide programs best suited to your course. The products you choose for these programs should be based on soil and tissue testing, as described in Chapter Two. Too often, however, in choosing products, superintendents are tempted to "go with what they know," products they're familiar with. Or they accept the recommendations of other area golf course superintendents and/or distributors. Or they are swayed by promotional materials of the latest fad products that promise superior results.

Without the scientific backing soil and tissue tests can provide, you will be merely guessing what will work for you. Once you know the nutritional needs of the soil and the plants, you can comfortably choose a brand of fertilizer that has the proper components to provide the necessary nutritional requirements.

Fertilizing for tournaments, especially greens, is all about being in control, so in addition to testing, the other important factor in choosing fertilizer and pest products is timing. Allow enough time to have the testing done and, subsequently, to evaluate and try various products to meet the specifications determined by the soil and tissue tests. When the date of the tournament is just around the corner it is not the time to be trying a new product or vendor. You need to know well in advance of that date, and before you apply any product, how much growth you are going to get once it has been put down, and how long it will remain active. This will allow you to gauge when to make the final application prior to the golf tournament. Consider the following:

- If your primary objective is to maintain a certain, consistent green speed throughout the day, but you are getting large amounts of growth each day, it will be very difficult to accomplish your objective.
- If you are looking for consistent green speed throughout the tournament week, and apply a fertilizer on Wednesday prior to tournament week, and its effects start fading the Thursday of that week, there will be a noticeable difference in green speed by the weekend.

## NOTE

Resist the temptation, or pressure from others, to underfertilize in order to gain green speed. The result is usually a thinned stand of turf on the green.

Also think about how granular products release. Water-soluble products don't provide long feeding periods, whereas coated products can feed for extremely long periods of time, depending on the type of coating. Keep in mind, too, that some fertilizers are dependent on water and temperature for their release. A superintendent I know used a product one spring to feed the turf until just prior to tournament time. That spring started out as very cool and dry; but then the weather changed about 10 days prior to the tournament, turning very warm and wet. The fertilizer he used was still present, and consequent to the change in the weather, it became activated. Needless to say the green speeds were greatly affected by this, and there was nothing the superintendent could do to slow the growth of the turf enough to help the green speed.

## Feeding Methods

The preferred method of fertilizing in preparation for golf tournaments is to use granular products in the spring and fall (unless tournament time falls at theses times) and switch to liquid applications during the prime golfing season. For superintendents in warmer climates, this may mean making only one or two applications of granular products in the spring before switching over to liquid applications.

The use of liquid fertilizers, also known as spoon-feeding, is a very effective way of controlling growth of the turfgrass plant. You apply just enough fertilizer to allow the plant to grow at a steady pace. Using the spoon-feeding method allows you to combine fertilizer applications with some pesticide applications, thereby saving time, money, and trips across the greens that are being prepared for the tournament. Some golf course superintendents spoon-feed their greens year-round, but I recommend caution when using this approach. Going back to the basics, remember that the turfgrass plant needs a certain amount of nitrogen per growing season, so make sure to add up the nitrogen you have applied to the greens and see if it falls within that range. If it does not, work in the necessary granular applications during the fall to make up the difference.

The best way to tell if the growth rate is correct is to monitor the amount of grass clippings in the mower baskets each morning. During prime golf season, the greens mowers should be picking up about one-fourth to one-third of a mower basket of grass per green. If you are mowing with triplex mowers, that would be the total after emptying all three baskets into one. This amount of growth gives you the maximum number of options when it comes to green speed. If the greens are getting too fast, the plants are growing enough that by skipping a mowing cycle, the green speed can be reduced to the desired speed; if they are too slow, you can simply add another mowing, or possibly just a rolling, or a combination of the two, to increase speed.

As you are feeding the turf, take special note of the phosphorus and potassium you are applying—record each application and do the calculations to determine their amounts.

- *Phosphorus* is beneficial for establishing new plants and for rooting during establishment; it is also important if your greens contain a high amount of sand, such as USGA and California-style greens. These high-sand-content greens tend to be deficient in phosphorus early in their lives, until they become well established and mature. That said, rare exceptions have been noted in which the native sand contained some phosphorus. This makes the argument for frequent soil testing even stronger.
- *Potassium* is an important element in regard to stress in the turfgrass plant. The recommended rate for potassium is now about 1:1 with the amount of nitrogen applied to the plant. Potassium enables the plant to better tolerate heat and drought stress, as well as traffic. When preparing a golf course for tournaments, potassium can make a major difference in how the course recovers after the event is over.

In addition to phosphorus and potassium, many other micronutrients play important roles in preparing turf for tournaments. For example:

- If your greens do not have the shade of green you would like, you can add iron applications to heighten the color.
- Silica applications have been shown in some cases to help with ball marks, by making the cell walls of the plants stronger and more resistant to the damage from the impact of golf balls.
- There are also many amino acid products and additives on the market. Again, test them well ahead of tournament preparation so that you know how the turf will react to them. Watch for the effects these products have on green speed. Some aid the plant in growth, which may have a negative impact on green speed.

FIGURE 3.6. SPRAYING GREENS REQUIRES ACCURACY AND THE PROPER EQUIPMENT.

Before using any of the mentioned products, make sure they are compatible with the other products you are spraying (Figure 3.6). Conduct a simple "jar test": mix together small samples of each product that you plan to spray and observe any adverse reactions. Run this test, too, if you are using a new formulation of products you have sprayed before.

*Applying Pesticides and Growth Regulators*

As with fertilizers, the key to pesticide applications during tournament preparation is to plan well ahead so that during the event the sprayer never has to leave the maintenance facility. Over the course of the year, take into consideration:

- Weed problems
- Disease problems
- Insect problems

- Wildlife problems (moles, voles, muskrats, geese, and any other animal)

Before undertaking any type of nuisance animal control, consult with the experts—your local wildlife authorities. It is usually advisable to plan your pesticide applications so that the last spray is made as late in the week prior to the tournament date as possible. If, however, it is a weekend-only tournament, it may be best to make the application the Monday or Tuesday prior to the event. This application would include any pesticides, fertilizers, or growth regulators, as needed.

A growth regulator is another tool you can use to help prepare your golf course for tournaments. These products work to slow the growth of the plant and assist you in "keeping a hand on the throttle." If you use growth regulators as part of your normal practices, experiment with the rates during the season so that when it comes time for the tournament you know exactly what rate to use and how long the effects of the product will last. During one application, use the product at the maximum label rate; next apply it at half rate; experiment with fractions in between. This will allow you to become more knowledgeable about the effects of the growth regulator and what to expect from it. For example, assume you are going into a stressful period, and you want a little more growth from the plant. By experimenting in this way, you may discover that going at a half rate and applying the regulator five days prior to the tournament, versus at the full rate seven days prior to the event, you can achieve the same results as it relates to green speed, yet still have some growth of the plant to help ease stress on the plant.

It's also essential that you learn how the different chemistries work. There are some sterile inhibitor fungicides that have growth regulation properties, which, when combined with certain growth regulators, can have detrimental results. If such combinations are applied in the heat of the summer, the plant will be less likely to recover from the mechanical and wear damage caused by daily maintenance and play.

The bottom line when it comes to chemical and growth regulator applications is to plan your program carefully and test it out when there is little or no stress on the turfgrass plant.

## WATER MANAGEMENT

Understandably, proper water management is becoming a more critical issue every year as water itself is becoming one of our most jeopardized resources. As a golf course superintendent, it behooves you to also be a good steward of the environment, and having a properly designed and functioning irrigation system will help you to save water, by applying only the amount necessary for healthy turf growth, avoiding saturated ground, and preventing runoff scenarios.

### Water Management Tools

There are many tools available to golf course superintendents that will help them manage water and, ultimately, the golf course maintenance budget (Figure 3.7). By properly using the tools

FIGURE 3.7. WATER MANAGEMENT TOOLS OF THE TRADE.

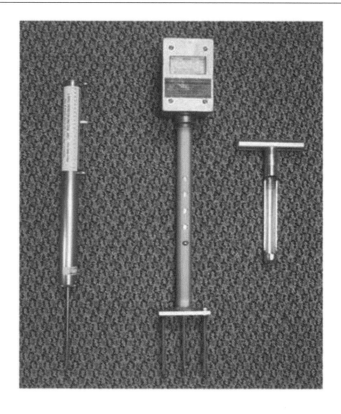

listed here, you can provide the firm, fast conditions that make
tournament golf exciting, consistent, and fair.

- Heads and nozzles
- Moisture sensors
- Computerized irrigation and weather stations
- Soil probe, for hand-watering
- Moisture meter
- Wetting agents

*Heads and nozzles:* No one head and nozzle arrangement is right
to use on the entire golf course. You will need a variety of combinations to achieve the most uniform watering results. For example, you will use circle heads in certain strategic locations,
adjustable arc nozzles in others, and high-volume nozzles in
some areas and low-volume nozzles in others.

*Moisture sensors:* As areas of dryness start to appear, you will want
to have on hand moisture sensors that will make it possible to
measure the moisture levels along the course. These are simple
to use: You insert the sensor into different areas of green and
take a reading from each, recording them as you go. This enables
you to compare areas with adequate moisture against drier sections. With these comparisons, you can then determine how
much water to add, and where. The instrument previously described is the Turf Tech Moisture Meter.

The Lang Penetrometer measures the firmness of the green
from area to area: Simply find an area that has the desired firmness and use that measure as the standard against which to compare all other sections of the green and from green to green to
achieve consistency.

*Computerized irrigation and weather stations:* No discussion on
water management tools would be complete without a mention
of computerized irrigation and weather stations, especially
evapotranspiration (ET). With these systems available, you
have the ability to fine-tune watering practices so that each
area of the golf course can receive the exact amount of water

necessary to help the turfgrass survive even in extremely dry conditions. Most of these systems have a weather station attached to them, to aid in determining how much water to apply to replace what was lost during the day due to wind, humidity, and rain.

As helpful as these tools are, they are not a substitute for taking regular trips around the golf course and implementing the other tools discussed in this section. Typically, there is only one weather station, and it is usually located convenient to the maintenance building, which is not necessarily the best position to record accurate weather data. Moreover, those golf courses that have housing additions surrounding them are usually so spread out that one weather station may not be enough to provide accurate readings for the entire course. Therefore, it is advisable to look at the recorded ET everyday but make the determination as to how much water to apply based on what you observe in the field. Remember, no irrigation system is perfect, and hand-watering will still need to be done.

*Soil probes:* When it comes to adding water by hand, one tool that all operators should have is a simple soil probe, which enables them to periodically check for moisture penetration. It is not uncommon to see individuals who have not been properly trained in this skill to apply too much water, causing excess puddling in the low area of the green, while preventing water in the dry area from penetrating.

*Wetting agents:* Wetting agents can also be used to help manage water use on a golf course. These products can be sprayed on using a boom sprayer, if the entire green or large areas need to be sprayed; or they can be applied using devices that attach to the end of the hose while the green is being hand-watered, if only the dry area needs to have the wetting agent applied.

To reap the maximum benefits of a wetting agent, it is advisable to thoroughly water it in after it is applied to the putting surface, and to do it early enough prior to tournaments so that the maximum benefit can be reaped.

## Overhead Irrigation

To repeat, the ideal conditions for tournament play are firm and fast. The objective is to reward a properly struck shot. At the same time, a shot that has been mishit should not "hold" on the putting surface because the green is too wet. How do you, as golf course superintendent, provide these conditions? Answer: an effective overhead irrigation system—with some help from Mother Nature (Figure 3.8). There is no perfect irrigation system, but there are ways to maximize the one you have.

- Start by identifying any shortcomings your current system may have, noting each as an item for inclusion on the plan you will devise to improve the system.
- Understand the environmental make-up of each individual green, and how that affects the way a green dries out—or does

Figure 3.8. Overhead Irrigation Must be Properly Managed to Produce Tournament-Quality Conditions.

not dry out. (Note that golf courses lose more grass due to excessively wet conditions than to dry conditions.)

• Examine the nozzles in the current irrigation heads. Are they the best nozzles for the area that needs to be covered?
• Consider replacing the irrigation heads, if there is a better head on the market that can give the type of coverage needed for any given green.

On every green that has a problem area, go through this process with an irrigation technician and your assistant. You may also want to seek the input from a local irrigation distributor or an irrigation design consultant to help resolve this type of issue.

Most problems related to irrigation issues occur because the staff, and in some instances the golf course superintendent, do not understand proper watering techniques. Much of the challenge of proper watering of greens comes when the tops of the undulations start to dry out during the day. The natural tendency, then, is to increase the run times on those stations. But what often happens when you resort to this practice is that the lower areas become too wet; the longer this goes on, the more saturated these areas become, until the turf starts to thin. The proper way to resolve this problem is by adding supplemental water through hand-watering (described in the next section).

---

## PROFESSIONAL TOURNAMENTS AND WATERING

Most superintendents think that the professional hosting bodies (PGA, USGA, LPGA, etc.) require that overhead irrigation systems not be used, and no water be applied, during tournaments. Nothing could be further from the truth. When tournament officials arrive, typically they find golf courses that are too wet. They then have to work with the golf course superintendent to produce a firm, fast golf course that results in a successful test of golf. The key is to find the happy medium, which generally means a golf course showing a little brown, but with turf healthy enough to recover quickly once the tournament is over. Again, this is tied to greens that are healthy (i.e., not overwatered) going into the tournament.

If the overhead irrigation must be used during the tournament period, it is advisable to turn it on only after all the players have left the property; and if it is done at night, assign staff to stay and monitor the system, watching for heads that "stick on" or do not rotate. This will save time the next morning when the grounds crew is preparing the course for the day's play—they won't be faced with repairing a washed-out bunker or pumping a flooded drain tile.

## HAND-WATERING

As mentioned in the previous section, hand-watering is an essential supplement to overhead irrigation when preparing a golf course for a tournament. To ensure it is done properly, you must teach members of the maintenance staff the art of hand-watering (Figures 3.9 and 3.10). It is also a good idea to train all other staff

FIGURE 3.9. HAND-WATERING IS A MUST TO TURN OUT TOURNAMENT-QUALITY PUTTING SURFACES.

FIGURE 3.10. HAND-WATERING IS AN ART, ONE THAT NEEDS TO BE TAUGHT AND
PRACTICED PRIOR TO HOLDING A TOURNAMENT.

members how to do this, so that in an emergency they can be
called on to help.

The ultimate goal of hand-watering is twofold: one as it relates to tournament golf (the competition side), the other as it
relates to healthy turf (the agronomic side):

- *Tournament golf:* The goal here is to help provide a uniform
  putting surface, one where the drier areas of turf are mois-
  tened by hand-watering until they have the same moisture level
  as the rest of the green. That way, as the ball rolls across these
  areas, it will not gain or lose speed.
- *Healthy turf:* Basic agronomic principles dictate hand-watering
  to add more water to those areas that tend to dry out more
  quickly or that may not receive adequate irrigation from the
  overhead sprinklers. The purpose is to ensure the turf will survive until conditions change and the drought stress placed on
  these areas subsides.

*Hand-Watering Tools*

Proper hand-watering, of course, requires the proper tools, in good condition. Therefore, in addition to training your staff, you must also take an accurate inventory of hoses and hose nozzles and verify they are in good operating order.

- Inspect hoses for repaired areas, where a band or barb may be protruding that will leave a scratch in the green surface if the hose is dragged across the green. (You might want to consider purchasing a hose that comes on a retractable reel in a vault, which can be buried around the green site, and so is always available. That way, if a staff member notices the need for additional irrigation, there is no need to return to the maintenance facility to get a hose.)
- Check nozzles that will be used on the green for a good pattern. If they are adjustable, check that the adjustment part of the nozzle is working and producing the proper spray pattern.
- Does the golf course have quick coupler attachments around the green, or must the operators plug into an irrigation head? If the former, operators must be properly trained how to open the irrigation head for access, and how to reassemble it so that it works properly the next time it must be used for overhead irrigation. If the golf course does not have quick couplers, I recommend that the cost of their installation be added to the irrigation budget.

## ACHIEVING TOURNAMENT PUTTING CONDITIONS

Another key component of a successful golf tournament is a smooth, consistent putting surface, one that lasts throughout the event. Achieving this objective requires consideration of these issues:

- Mowing style
- Mowing height
- Precision maintenance
- Smoothness of the green surface

- Firmness of the green surface
- Other areas of concern

## MOWING STYLE

In choosing between walk mowing and triplex mowing to prepare greens for tournament play, walk mowing is the preferred method (Figure 3.11), although triplex mowing has its benefits, too.

### Walk Mowing

With walk mowing, the quality of cut you can achieve is unmatched, and the smaller lines result in a very aesthetically pleasing look. With the roller directly behind the cutting unit, after the turf has been cut, the putting surface receives an effective roll, producing a smooth, clean appearance. Moreover, the weight

FIGURE 3.11. WALK MOWING IS THE PREFERRED METHOD FOR PRODUCING TOP-QUALITY PUTTING SURFACES.

of the unit helps the roller to be effective, as opposed to the small, lightweight rollers that are attached to the cutting units on the triplex mower.

There are many top-quality walk mowers on the market today. Which one should you buy? Talk with your local distributors and test the various models on your golf course. If you have undulating greens, pay close attention to how the mower goes over the contours. Does it scalp? Or does it roll smoothly across, leaving a nice even surface? Solicit feedback from your operators about user comfort, ease of turning, and the ability to mow a straight line. Don't neglect to talk with your mechanic about serviceability, and factor in those remarks with your own field observations and price considerations.

How many walking mowers should you have on hand when preparing for a golf tournament? Ten is a comfortable number for an 18-hole golf course. Most of the time there will be four mowing the front nine, four mowing the back nine, and two mowing the practice areas. If the greens are being double-cut, this gives the maintenance staff plenty of time to get the job done without being rushed. It's also a good idea to have one or two back-up mowers in the shop, just in case one breaks down or has a quality-of-cut issue that cannot be quickly resolved in the field. Keep in mind that walking greens mowers are the choice for cutting collars as well, so when it comes time to take an inventory of the current mowers, request additional units from vendors.

When actually mowing the greens, it is critical to ensure that the height of cut on all the mowers be set the same (except in cases where a mower is set at a slightly higher height or has a different roller on it, to alleviate stress). Remember that there is a difference between the true height of cut and bench setting. Two greens mowers that are set at the same bench height may not mow at exactly the same height of cut in the field, especially if they are made by different manufacturers. So, when teaming mowers to mow the same green, make sure that you team the same brand of machines together. Likewise, the weight of the units will vary from manufacturer to manufacturer, and if you mix different-weight mowers on one green, a portion of the green may actually putt differently from the other part. The difference may be slight but enough to be noticed by some of the better

FIGURE 3.12A.  THE PRISM GAUGE GIVES THE TRUE CUTTING HEIGHT, AS WELL AS
A PICTURE OF THE QUALITY OF CUT.

players. One tool that will help achieve a consistent cut height in the field is the prism gauge (Figures 3.12A and 3.12B). This instrument will allow you and the mechanic to get a clear picture of the height at which a greens mower is actually cutting on the green. It will also demonstrate how cleanly the grass is being cut.

*Triplex Mowing*

Triplex mowing is a good option for tournaments that are held early or late in the season, when the maintenance staff may not be in full force. With qualified operators working, two triplexes can do the job of five or six walking greens mowers, thereby freeing up staff members to help perform other jobs that are just as important in making the tournament a success. Certainly, the triplex mowers available on the market today can give you a very good-quality-cut. But caution must be taken if the putting surface

FIGURE 3.12B. CLOSE-UP VIEW OF A PRISM GAUGE.

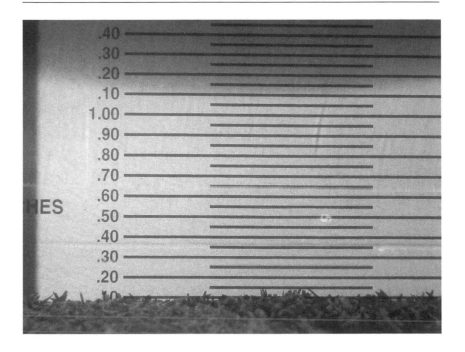

is either wet or soft, because these mowers tend to leave tire tracks, which precludes achieving and maintaining a smooth surface. This is especially true if the operator uses a triplex mower to do the clean-up pass and goes over the same area day after day; grooves will inevitably start to appear in the area, which may also start to thin out due to compaction. So, if you are going to use a triplex mower for the clean-up pass, do so only every other day. A better idea still is to use a walking greens mower for this purpose.

Another downside to triplex mowers is the noise factor. Unless the models being used are electric, they produce substantially more noise than walk mowers. From an operational standpoint, this could be a problem if greens and tees are in proximity of each other, or if the driving range and practice green areas are close to a green or tee. In this case, you may need to reroute the mowers so that there are no machines in the immediate area as participants are warming up (Figure 3.13).

Figure 3.13. Although Triplex Mowing Can Produce Good Putting Surfaces, Hand-Mowing is Preferred for Tournament Purposes.

## Mowing Height

Mowing height is the last area to adjust when determining how to accomplish the desired green speed. If the cutting height is producing a decent speed for normal daily play, and the greens need to roll faster for a tournament, or the membership is not happy with the daily speed, look first at factors such as rolling, topdressing, verticutting, and double-cutting, before lowering the height of cut.

You, the golf course superintendent—not management—should decide the cutting height for the greens, based on factors such as:

• Proper cutting height for the type and variety of grass on the putting green, as recommended by Dr. James Beard, President and Chief Scientist International SportsTurf Institute and Professor Emeritus of Turfgrass Science, Texas A&M University, and other noted agronomists.

- Area where the putting green is located, starting with the geographic location and ending with the microclimate.
- Amount of play the putting green receives each year and during stressful times.
- Level of ability of the players putting on the greens. Remember, many people play golf purely for the enjoyment of the game, and greens that roll too fast may dilute their experience.
- Budget set for the golf course, and the ability of the golf facility to provide the tools and equipment necessary to maintain the greens at the cutting height prescribed.
- Height that will enable the golf course superintendent to grow healthy turfgrass.

## PRECISION MAINTENANCE

As the leader of the golf course staff, you must be vigilant that every job is being done with precision when preparing a golf course for a tournament, paying special attention to greens maintenance and preparation. From the mechanic working on the equipment to the operator in the field, overlook nothing and no one.

Verify that the greens mowers are set correctly, and that each adjustable area on the mower is set with precision. The old height gauges—where an adjustment screw was set to a certain height, slid onto the bedknife, laid across the rollers, and then slid back and forth to "feel" if the setting was accurate—cannot compare to today's dial gauges that read in the hundred-thousandths of an inch. Years ago, when the greens were being cut at 3/16 of an inch, these gauges served the golf course superintendent well; but today, when greens are being cut at an 1/8 of an inch or less, the dial gauges give you and the mechanic the precision necessary to provide the accuracy for the quality of cut that is demanded in the field.

Take care, and be precise, when it comes to backlapping greens mowers and choosing replacement reels and bedknives. Work with your mechanic to ensure that the replacement parts (reels and bedknives) you purchase produce quality results in the field. For example, an original manufacturer's reel combined with an aftermarket bedknife may not produce a precision cut. There have been instances where the metals of the two were not compatible and produced a rippling effect on the green. Locate sources for the appropriate parts well in advance of any tournament dates so that if changes need to be made during the event they can be installed with confidence.

Precision performance must be required, as well, of your staff assigned to mowing operations. They must learn how to take a quick walk over the green, checking for foreign materials, such as a spike that has fallen out of a pair of golf shoes, sticks or small stones from bunkers that will cause damage to a reel and bed-knife. The same can be said of a small twig or leaf that becomes caught in the edge of the mower and dragged across the green, leaving a scratch mark that could possibly change the direction of a golf ball rolling across the green. The maintenance staff must understand how important these little things can be when preparing the golf course for a tournament. From a time standpoint alone, they mean a lot. Many times these problems occur when staff members are hurrying to ready the golf course for a shotgun start, or when they are double-cutting and can barely stay ahead of play. But as always with mistakes, it takes longer to correct them than to prevent them. More important, in terms of the tournament itself, is that if the mistakes are not corrected by the time the first group plays the hole, but are subsequently corrected, the course of play has potentially been altered—that is, the green could putt differently for one group or player than for another.

Precision is a must, too, for the operator cutting the clean-up pass. The clean-up area needs to be established weeks ahead of the tournament, by defining the edge of the collar and the putting green. A uniform collar on every hole is very important, and is easy to create. Simply take two pieces of wood, one to be used as a handle and the other measured to the desired width of the collar, usually around 30 inches, and mounted to the handle. Next you—the superintendent—or a trusted assistant superintendent with good turf knowledge should identify the grass that is to be in the collar (in northern climates, usually where the bentgrass meets the grass used for the rough around the green), then set the measuring stick down; finally, apply a dot of paint to each end of the measuring stick (Figure 3.14). Do this about every two steps until a

FIGURE 3.14. TOOLS TO DOT COLLARS.

complete circle is made around the green. Once the dots have been placed around the green, it is important to instruct the greens mowers to mow over the dots at the green/collar interface, and the collar mowers to mow over the dots at the collar/ rough interface. This is most important at the green/collar interface, because the definition must be obvious so that the player can determine whether the golf ball is on the green or in the collar. If the ball is on the green, the golfer has certain options, such as marking the ball and cleaning it; if the ball is in the collar, it must be played as it lies, although the player has the option of leaving the flagstick in the hole. The more clearly you explain the importance of these details to the maintenance staff, the better job they will do in performing their jobs.

## SMOOTHNESS OF THE GREEN SURFACE

Tournament players expect a smooth putting surface that rolls true—meaning a ball rolls on the green and breaks toward the hole just the way the player "reads" it will. The two main areas you can work on to produce smooth, true rolling greens are: (1) to control grain, which aids in the true roll; and (2) rolling, which leads to the smooth surface.

For tournament preparation, greens are rolled for smoothness, not firmness (see the next section on achieving firmness). It is always best to roll after mowing; and if the greens are becoming too fast for tournament play, it is best to skip a mowing, but continue to roll to help keep the greens smooth.

There are many good rollers on the market. Some are designed so that the operator sits on the machine and rides as it rolls side to side (Figure 3.15); others are set up as replacements for the reels on triplex greens mowers (these can also be set up to vibrate); still others are pushed across the green by hand (Figure 3.16). Each type of roller has its advantages and disadvantages. The main thing you must determine is which kind of roller is best

FIGURE 3.15. A RIDING GREENS ROLLER IS USED TO SMOOTH THE PUTTING SURFACE.

FIGURE 3.16. A HAND ROLLER USED FOR SMOOTHING GREENS.

for the particular type of greens and golf course it will be used on. Greens with very narrow turning areas may make it impossible to use triplex rollers, in which case hand rollers may be the best choice. Extremely large greens, in contrast, would be best served by one of the riding rollers.

## FIRMNESS OF THE GREEN SURFACE

Putting green surfaces for tournament play must be smooth and true, as just discussed, as well as firm. Firm means that when you walk on the green it does not have a spongy feel. When a properly struck ball is hit from the fairway onto a green that is firm, it will stop; conversely, a poorly struck ball hit from the fairway or rough onto a firm green will not stop. How do you go about providing a firm putting surface? The best way is to establish a good cultural practices program, as discussed previously. To help alleviate the spongy feeling, make sure that thatch is kept to a minimum, by core-aerifying on a regular schedule and making light, frequent applications of topdressing every two to three weeks.

Too often, golf course superintendents—and many avid tournament fans—think the best way to provide firm surfaces is to cut off water to the greens completely during the period leading up to and during tournament play. Contrary to this belief, a good water management plan—controlling the amount of water that is being put down—is the best way to provide firm greens. Specifically, supply just enough moisture to get the greens through to the next watering cycle, and supplement by hand-watering the areas that dry out.

One tool you can use to gauge the firmness of the greens is the Lang Penetrometer. First, determine when the greens have the desired firmness, and take a measurement with the Lang Penetrometer, so that you have an accurate reading of that level in your records. Then, as tournament time approaches, begin to use the Lang Penetrometer on a daily basis to maintain the desired firmness.

By incorporating good cultural practices, controlled watering practices, and using a measuring device, you and your staff can provide a putting surface that is firm yet fair to the tournament players.

## OTHER AREAS OF CONCERN

A number of other areas inevitably require attention on or around the green prior to the tournament date. Addressing these areas and fixing any problems are all part of good greens management practices. Typical other areas of concern are:

- Collar-to-green definition
- Thin areas to repair and protect
- Bad cup plugs

A word of warning here: If left unaddressed, these areas may sometimes seem to improve on their own, but don't count on it. In any case, if left alone, they will never be as good as they could be if properly repaired before an event. When scheduling repairs to these areas, remember to allow time for healing, especially if sodding is involved. Ideally, when sodding, you must lay it early enough to give the seams time to grow over completely and to ensure that the sod has rooted well enough to handle the traffic and light to moderate drought, so that it does not need to be hand-watered during the event.

### Collar-to-Green Definition

I've discussed collar-to-green definition earlier in the chapter, but I bring it up again here because of its importance and because this is something that must be done when the weather dictates; it cannot be put off until the week prior to the tournament.

For example, if the collar width is not uniform, and there is great disparity, it will take many mowings with slight increment changes to ensure that the desired height is reached without scalping the area. It may also require a walking greens mower to be set up on a bevel for a period of time to lower one portion of the collar while keeping the rest of the collar at a desired height.

### Thin Areas to Repair and Protect

Also time-sensitive is the repair or sodding necessary to improve thin areas on the putting surface or around the green. Allow plenty of time to enable healing prior to the event. If sodding is done, make sure that the new sod matches up with the edges of the old sod, to prevent bumps that may deflect a golf ball as it rolls over the area (Figure 3.17). If the repaired area is just off the putting surface, do it early enough to ensure that the sod has "knitted" enough so that a shot can be properly played from it. There is a rule (USGA Rules of Golf: Ground Under Repair: Appendix I, Section E) that can be instituted for relief from sodded areas, but it is better to do the repair rather than invoke the rule.

Keep in mind, too, seasonal changes to putting surfaces. When the weather is good early in the season, the turf will grow well and look and play the way it should; but as the season progresses and the normal stresses of the growing season occur, areas will start to thin out—usually around the collars of the green or just outside the green collar, where mower or foot traffic seem to compound the stress. You must protect these areas. Collars are easily protected using sheets of plywood or even rubber

Figure 3.17. When Laying Sod on a Putting Surface, Do It Well in Advance of Any Tournament, and Take Care to Ensure Proper Results.

doormats, with the carpet side placed against the turf and the rubber side up (Figure 3.18). Don't forget to explain to the maintenance staff why these materials must be used. When you and the staff begin to implement these procedures well in advance of tournament time, you can protect those areas that typically thin out so that they are in the condition they need to be in to meet the demands of the players.

*Bad Cup Plugs*

Another important issue requiring attention is bad cup plugs. Unfortunately, they tend to turn up in areas ideal for tournament hole locations, because often they are the choice spots on the green for member play.

It is not uncommon for three or more bad (i.e., high, scalped, or low) cup plugs to appear on the same green. If these plugs are repaired when first noticed (ideally, the day they are changed), it may be possible to avoid scalping the high plugs. It is important

FIGURE 3.18. GREENS MOWERS TURNING ON MATS TO ALLEVIATE STRESS ON THE COLLAR.

to train cup cutters in the proper techniques of repairing the cup plug. (This technique will be discussed in Chapter Six.)

Greens mower operators, too, must be aware of the cup plug, and check it for proper depth prior to mowing over it, if there is any question that it may not be right. You might want to assign an assistant superintendent or a crew leader to identify and mark with a dot of paint any cup plugs that need to be repaired and then send one or two cup cutters out to do the repairs. By putting all these checks and balances in place, it becomes easier to correct the problem of high and low cup plugs. Here, too, make these repairs well in advance of the tournament, as it may take up to 21 days for a repaired plug to fully heal.

## SUMMARY

Many factors must come together to produce a top-quality putting surface for tournament play. Every detail must be thought out and planned for, from the green speed to the maintenance of the equipment that will be used to produce the quality putting surface. Work closely with the maintenance staff, to ensure they are aware of the importance of every aspect of the maintenance operation. They must become confident in their ability to produce the conditions prescribed by you and the golf committee. That confidence is gained by repeated practice of all maintenance operations.

To reiterate all we've covered in this chapter:

- Your ability to control thatch and grain on the putting surface will lead to putts that roll smooth and true.
- Reaching the speed goal set during the planning process is a result of proper topdressing techniques, fertilization practices, and the appropriate cutting height for the turfgrass species.
- Using proper cultural practices and maintaining all of the cutting equipment will help to produce a quality cut and reduce scalping when the cutting height must be lowered.

In sum, by setting and following proper maintenance standards for the golf course for the entire season, by tournament time you should only need to tweak a few cutting heights to make the course ready to host a highly successful event.

# Chapter Four

# Tees, Fairways, and Roughs

In a typical round of golf, half of the shots are played on or around the greens yet they typically encompass on average only 2 to 5 acres of the entire golf course. That is why so much attention, time, and money are spent on greens management. That is not to say that the tees, fairways, and roughs where the remainder of the game is played are any less important. In this chapter we will look at managing those areas in the same healthy manner we manage greens so that when it is time for any tournament we may be hosting the entire golf course will be ready.

## Tees

When it comes to tournament play, especially local club events, the most important areas, and those usually remembered best by golfers, are the putting greens. That said, the tees at many courses are just as important. The players need a good place to start from on each hole, and the teeing ground is that place.

The first tee, in particular, makes a statement about the golf course, thus making it an important focus of maintenance. On many courses, the first tee is the only one to show a significant amount of wear, and to have numerous bare areas. There are various reasons for this: the tee is too small; players often hit two balls from the first tee; there is usually a lot of congestion around the first tee, caused by the players, starters giving instructions, and groups watching each other tee off and discussing the games they will play that day. Typically, there's also more landscaping decoration in the area, in the form of flower beds and other features.

By paying special attention to the construction of the first tee, the golf course architect and the builder can give the golf course superintendent a head start when it comes to maintaining a well-conditioned first teeing area, which can set the tone for the players' tournament experience. To maintain quality teeing surfaces, the following topics are of particular significance:

- Levelness
- Size
- Firmness
- Areas requiring protection
- Obstructions
- Distance and alignment

## LEVELNESS

To get off to a great start on each hole, the golfer must execute a properly hit tee shot. To do this, a level playing surface is required. This can be a real challenge for some superintendents, depending on how old their golf course is; on older courses, the tees may have a slight tilt (slope), for drainage purposes. This type of tilt is acceptable as long as it is slight and extends over the entire length of the tee. If the tees are soil tees, and were tilted for drainage purposes during construction, the preferred tilt is higher in the front and lower in the rear. If at all possible, there should be no tilt from side to side, as this can cause the golfer to slice or hook the ball. If the teeing surfaces are constructed of a clay base with a sand root-zone mix, the tees may be perfectly level at the base and top, with drain tile installed in a pattern similar to a putting green. Another method of tee construction is to use a modified root-zone mix and slope the clay base to the center, then install a drain tile down the center of the tee to carry the water off; the teeing surface will be perfectly flat with the modified root-zone mix.

Periodically verify the evenness of the teeing surfaces using a level; and if any settling has occurred, identify and note those areas for later correction. On those teeing areas that have settled or become unlevel over time, use all the resources necessary to make the proper adjustments. The entire area of the tee that needs leveling must be stripped, along with an additional area back into the level area of the tee, to ensure a proper transition with no bumps. If the uneven area is small and raised, it may be possible to level it with a series of hollow-tine aerification, followed by rolling with a moderately heavy roller. If the area is low, it will be necessary to remove the sod and raise the area with soil or root-zone mix.

As with most pretournament maintenance procedures, you'll have to do this well ahead of the tournament date, so that the sod will knit and the seams will disappear, especially when the area will be used for the tournament.

## Size

Superintendents in charge of older facilities may have tees that are somewhat small, and built to handle the amount of play at the time when they were constructed (see Figure 4.1). As the

FIGURE 4.1. SMALL TEES CAN CREATE MAINTENANCE PROBLEMS THAT REQUIRE REBUILDING OF THE TEE IN ORDER TO SOLVE THE PROBLEM.

game of golf has grown and changed, many of these courses are now having difficulty accommodating the increase in rounds. The result is these facilities are having problems maintaining healthy turf on the tees because there is not enough time for recovery of the turf before the area must be used again. Nowhere is this more evident than on the par three tees. It is common to find par three tees with less space than on many of the par fours and fives. The shorter the par three, the more this becomes a problem, because on the shorter par threes there are more golfers taking a divot, without adequate time for divot recovery. However, the older golf courses are not the only ones with this problem; many of the newly constructed tees use a free-form design and incorporate several levels of teeing ground, many of which are very small and do not hold up well under heavy play and intense weather conditions (rain, drought, etc.). Consequently, many golf course superintendents find it advantageous to eliminate the tiers and combine the space to make one larger tee. If you face this problem, be sure to consult with the golf course architect before you make any changes to the golf course. Explain the difficulty and ask for expert help in resolving the problem. If the course is under construction, take special care to ensure that all of the tees are of adequate size; and if they are not, fix them during construction, the most cost-effective time to have them reshaped.

## FIRMNESS

Golfers playing tournaments like to have firm footing so they can take the necessary aggressive swing without fear of slipping. To establish a quality teeing ground for golfers, in general and especially for tournament play, firm tees are required. The way to achieve this goal is to follow the cultural practices discussed earlier in the book to produce healthy turf. To review:

- Timely aerifications need to occur when optimal growth will result, thereby ensuring quick healing and minimal disruption to play.
- A quality topdressing program will also be required, to help minimize thatch, ensure levelness, and promote growth and

divot recovery. Use of verticut units, as needed, to help reduce thatch is a must, as well.

It is vital that these practices be kept up to date on the forward tees, as well as on the back tees, even though, typically, the latter do not receive as much play. The back tees tend to become very soft and puffy, and so do not lend themselves well to tournament golf. Following these practices also leads to a healthier turf-grass plant.

In terms of topdressing tee divots during tournaments, you may want to hold off filling the divots, especially if the same area of the tee will be used again in subsequent rounds. Topdressing divots with loose sand may cause golfers to slip as they rotate through the golf ball. However, if the tee area will be moved to one where the golfers will not be standing in freshly topdressed divots, this becomes a nonissue.

## Areas Requiring Protection

You may find it necessary to protect certain areas that will be used for the competition, to ensure there is adequate grass on the teeing surface. Take time to plan for the entire tournament, keeping in mind that if it is two, three, or four days in duration, many areas (or square footage) may need to be covered. A number of good fabrics are available on the market today for this purpose (Figure 4.2). Any that will allow air and sunlight to pass through are acceptable. Nettings, made of plastic mesh with squares about half to three-quarters of an inch, work very well in allowing light and air to penetrate, while discouraging golfers to walk on or hit from the covered area.

Various areas may need to be protected, in particular, par threes or short par fours, where golfers may elect to hit an iron off the tee. If a particular hole is prone to changes in wind direction, thus play longer, you may choose to protect the tees that are intended for use, as well as an area that will make the hole play from a longer or shorter yardage, depending on the direction of the wind. In general, it is not recommended that you cover the farthest point to the rear of the tee; instead, allow the golfers to practice from this area so that they can play the hole from its most distant point.

FIGURE 4.2. MANY DIFFERENT MATERIALS ARE AVAILABLE TO PROTECT TEES, INCLUDING FABRICS AND PLASTIC SNOW FENCING.

## OBSTRUCTIONS

As noted in Chapter One, while conducting your course inventory, be on the lookout for low-hanging branches over teeing areas (Figure 4.3). Also be aware of tees located in "shoots," where the trees have grown in on each side of the tee, resulting in a very narrow space through which to direct the tee shot. Remove low-hanging branches, as well as any trees that may cause a condition that is less than fair to the players. If possible, refer to the architectural drawings to understand the architect's original intent for the tee shot. It is not uncommon to discover that when trees were planted, their growth pattern was not considered or not understood; thus, over time, the tree has become an obstruction, rendering part of the tee unusable for play. Sometimes, more than half the tee becomes unusable, resulting in tees that have very little grass on one side and near-perfect conditions on

FIGURE 4.3. DURING THE GOLF COURSE INVENTORY LOOK FOR
OBSTRUCTIONS THAT MAY INTERFERE WITH TEE SHOTS, SUCH AS
LOW-HANGING BRANCHES.

the other side. As previously recommended in the discussion on greens, in areas of high tree concentration, analyze how much morning sun penetrates to the turf surface. If that amount is less than desirable, resulting in poor turf conditions, consider removing one or more trees to correct this condition.

## DISTANCE AND ALIGNMENT

New technologies, coupled with greater athleticism, means that today's golfers can hit the ball farther. Therefore, many golf courses are considering adding distance to their facilities. If your course is one of those that has the ability and the money to do this, begin by consulting with a golf course architect, to assure that the new tee will perform to, and meet the expectations of, the club and its members.

For starters, the directors of the club should decide on the goals for the addition, then work with the architect to ensure that the proposed construction can meet those goals. For golf courses that do not have the ability or resources to lengthen the golf course, an option is to narrow fairways or adjust hazards to make the golf course more competitive. Here, too, before making any adjustments, set goals for the proposal and consult a golf course architect.

When constructing new tees, it is critical that the builder pay attention to their alignment (Figure 4.4). Tees must align with the fairway landing area or the green. Misalignment will result in difficulties for the maintenance staff when it comes to tee marker placement and mowing; it will also cause difficulties for the average golfer when it comes to aligning to the fairway for the tee shot. To ensure proper tee marker alignment, consider making a "T" out of PVC pipe so that staff members who set the tee markers

FIGURE 4.4. WHEN ADDING NEW TEES, MAKE SURE THEY ARE PROPERLY ALIGNED AND ACCOMPLISH THE GOALS SET FOR THEM.

will have a reference tool to help them align the tee markers to the center of the landing area or green. When mowing tees for regular maintenance, it is advisable to mow in four different directions, similar to mowing greens. For tournament mowing, specifically, it is best to mow straight toward the landing area or green. This gives the best appearance (especially if the event will be televised) and aids the golfer in lining up the tee shot, serving as a reference point for the center of the landing area.

# FAIRWAYS

Fairways make up the largest area of finely maintained turf on most golf courses. Considerable time and money is spent on keeping fairways in tournament-ready condition, and requires attention to many factors:

* Width
* Drainage
* Firmness
* General turfgrass health
* Mowing height and contouring
* Problems

## WIDTH

Deciding on the width of golf course fairways can be a difficult task. Many factors must be thought through prior to setting or adjusting fairway widths, so work with your golf professional and a golf course architect when making this decision.

The major deciding factor is the caliber of player who normally plays the golf course. If this person is a high handicapper, wider fairways may be advisable; but if the majority of play comes from low handicappers, they may enjoy the challenge of tight, narrow fairways. If, however, you must accommodate both levels of player, one option is to have a fairway that is wider at the beginning of the landing area, to help the higher-handicap players, while tapering in the fairway to a narrower expanse, to challenge the lower-handicap players. This approach can be a challenge, however, if the golf course is set up with multiple tees that attempt to tighten up the driving distance differences between the higher- and lower-handicap players.

When making changes to the width of the fairway, timing is critical. It must be done slowly, over time, so that the turf being lowered is not scalped. If the fairway is being narrowed, timing is less important. Of course, whether you're widening or narrowing, the transition must be complete prior to any tournament.

Another issue here is grass species. If the species are different in the area being narrowed or widened, you may have to strip off the current sod and install new sod of the desired species. That task is time-sensitive as well.

## DRAINAGE

Over time, drainage issues tend to appear in fairways. They cover large areas, and drainage patterns sometimes change due to variations that occur in elevations, caused by construction, aerification, and other maintenance practices. You may find, for example, that areas that once surface-drained very quickly now take several hours, or even days, to dry out completely. Or catch basins that cleared themselves rapidly now drain slowly and back up water on the fairways. Sometimes the catch basins, especially if they are smaller in diameter, will become covered over with grass, making them drain slower. While conducting the golf course inventory, make sure to examine all catch basins for any that are in danger of being grassed over. Grass-covered basins not only create a drainage problem but also raise safety issues. A golfer could unknowingly strike a golf ball that was on top of a covered catch basin and break a golf club or, worse, a wrist.

As wet areas appear, add new drainage to help them drain quickly. If an area already has drainage installed but it is still staying wet, investigate the reason why and correct it as soon as possible so that future problems will not arise in the same area. The area can then be maintained like the rest of the golf course fairways.

## FIRMNESS

Fairways must always remain firm and play fast, just as the rest of the golf course. To meet this objective, you must include a regular aerification program in the cultural practices of the golf course, as described throughout the book so far. If possible, aerify

the fairways at least twice per year, and you will see beneficial results very quickly; if you can aerify more than two times per year,
you will see even quicker results. Superintendents who aerify only
once per year, or not at all, usually must deal with frequent problems on their fairways.

It is also becoming common practice to topdress fairways with
sand for tournament preparation. Although this can be a very
expensive and time-consuming task, for those golf courses that
can afford it, it is very beneficial. Golf courses that have money in
the budget to topdress fairways, but not enough to do the entire
fairway, may elect to do just the landing and approach areas that
lead up to the green. This practice will also help maintain the firmness of the fairways, which will help you achieve one of the conditioning goals of tournament preparation. Other cultural practices,
such as verticutting, will aid in achieving proper firmness, as well.

Another way to promote firmness is to control the amount of
water that is applied through the irrigation system. If drainage is
working properly, and the amount of irrigation water applied is
in check with what the plant needs, maintaining firm fairways
should be no problem. Fairways that are dryer and firmer will
resist injury from mowing stress, cart traffic, and disease. This
approach to fairway firmness will also produce the fast playing
conditions that tournament golfers look for.

## General Turfgrass Health

Good general turf health is as important on fairways as on greens
and tees. Proper fertilization, pest control, and cultural practices
must be implemented throughout the growing season to produce
a healthy turfgrass plant. And if your golf course is located in a
northern climate or an area where turfgrass growth slows or ceases
for a period of time, you must take special care to give the plant
everything it needs to make it through this period and emerge
healthy when growing conditions become favorable again.

General health practices should include the following:

- Implement general fertilization practices similar to those you
  use on greens and tees. Apply only enough nitrogen to keep
  the plant healthy and produce enough growth so that divot recovery can occur in a reasonable amount of time. Remember

that the turf plant requires a certain amount of nitrogen per growing season, and staying in that range while controlling growth takes a very well-planned fertilization program.

Use a good mixture of granular and liquid fertilizers on the fairways, as you do on greens. Include minor elements such as iron, calcium, magnesium, and manganese matching recommendations from soil-testing results.

- Conduct pest control practices according to the needs of the turf, and as dictated by the environment and level of pressure from pests. You need to be the local expert when it comes to diseases, insects, and pests that attack turfgrass plants on the golf course. Take a preventative approach here: know the best way and time to address all pest activities.

- Include cultural practices such as core aerification, verticutting, and topdressing at the proper times during the growing season. Remember that turf under stress will incur further damage if cultural practices are performed at the wrong time. For example, if the fairway turf is stressed, delay the cultural practices until the environmental conditions once again favor growth and speedy recovery.

## MOWING HEIGHT AND CONTOURING

One of the major factors in achieving good turf health, as well as optimum playing conditions, is proper turf height on the fairways. Fairway turf height should fall within the range of recommended cutting heights for the species of grass on the fairways for tournament play. (Refer to the table below).

| Turfgrass Species | Height of Cut Range for Fairways |
| --- | --- |
| Bentgrass | .375″ to .500″ |
| Annual bluegrass | .438″ to .500″ |
| Kentucky bluegrass | .500″ to .750″ |
| Fine fescues | .500″ to .750″ |
| Ryegrass | .438″ to .500″ |
| Bermudagrass | .375″ to .500″ |
| Kikuyugrass | .438″ to .500″ |
| Paspalum | .375″ to .500″ |
| Zoysiagrass | .438″ to .500″ |

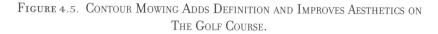

Figure 4.5. Contour Mowing Adds Definition and Improves Aesthetics on The Golf Course.

Most average golfers prefer the height of cut on fairways to be a little bit higher than those heights typically used for tournaments, so that it is easier for them to hit the shot that is required. This is especially the case with higher-handicap golfers who generally struggle with very low-cut turf and tight lies.

Proper contouring of the fairways is important to establish definition of the fairways, as well as to give golfers a pleasing view that will help them understand the proper way to play the golf hole (Figure 4.5). Contour mowing will help fairway bunker complexes stand out; this draws the golfer's eye to the bunkers, and the player must then make the decision to hit the ball away from the bunkers or to challenge them (Figure 4.6).

## Problems

A number of areas on the fairway are prone to problems. Pay close attention to the following as you conduct your course inventory; note and repair them as soon as possible.

FIGURE 4.6. PROPER CONTOUR DEFINITION HELPS SHOW THE GOLFER WHERE TO
HIT THE GOLF BALL; THE EFFECT IS VISUALLY PLEASING, AS WELL.

- Look for catch basins that may be covered over, may have cracked lids, or may be uneven.
- Keep an eye out for sprinkler heads that are damaged, partially covered over, or that have worn or damaged nozzles. Repair these quickly to prevent uneven distribution of water.
- Watch for holes where golfers tend to hit shots in a small area and take many divots. These are areas that may need to be protected (similar to tee areas) prior to tournaments.
- Check for drain lines or irrigation trenches that have settled over time; level these to prevent ruling issues. These can be repaired best by stripping the sod over the area, filling the area with soil, tamping, and then replacing the sod.
- Keep up with divot repair. Pay particular attention to holes where the approach shot comes from a small concentrated area, or on holes where golfers tend to use a shorter, more lofted club and take a bigger divot. For topdressing divots in fairways, it is important to use a good mix of sand, topsoil, and peat. Instruct the maintenance staff to fill the divots so that they are level; caution them against either over- or underfilling them.

The objective is to give a golfer whose ball lands on the filled divot a chance to hit the shot with some control, as if he/she were hitting from fairway turfgrass. When over- or underfilling or using straight sand in the divots, the golfer does not have control and is penalized for landing the ball in the fairway and ending up in an old divot.

# Roughs

The rough is an area of turf where the golfer is penalized for an errant shot. For the rough to cost the golfer the penalty shot, it must be well maintained just like the rest of the golf course. Unfortunately, the rough can be extremely challenging for the golf course superintendent, because when budgets are tight the rough is often chosen as the most likely area on which to save money. The rough is also where most high handicappers spend a majority of their time, so from a playability aspect it presents a challenge as well.

Your challenge, as superintendent, is to make the rough difficult enough that it costs the lower handicapper for an errant shot, but not so difficult that the higher-handicap player cannot advance the ball when hitting a recovery shot. To meet these seemingly contradictory goals—making the rough challenging yet fair—be sure to communicate with the golf professional and tournament committee to get a better understanding of the skill level(s) of the golfers who will be playing in the event.

To achieve a fair yet challenging rough, you must address the following:

- Density
- Mowing height and mower type
- Natural versus maintained rough
- Intermediate rough
- Obstructions

## Density

Density is defined as a measure of the number of aerial grass shoots per unit area. In greens management you are looking for turf density to provide a smooth, uniform putting surface; in the rough, you are looking for density that will provide a challenge to players attempting to recover from an errant shot.

Density can vary greatly among turfgrass species, and even among cultivars (Figures 4.7 to 4.9). Other factors also influence density: mowing height, fertilization practices, and cultural practices. A good, dense rough is produced when fertility requirements for the turf species are met on an annual basis, coupled with mowing practices that keep pace with the growth of the turf. To maintain density, it is also important to meet the water requirements of the turf. On golf courses with irrigated roughs, it is easier to maintain consistent density throughout the year. But many golf course roughs are not irrigated, making it more difficult to meet this objective year-round. During periods of adequate rainfall, the roughs will be lush and full, but once the drier season starts and the rainfall diminishes, the roughs will start to thin and lose much of their density. Even those golf courses with

FIGURE 4.7.  A THIN ROUGH CAN HINDER SUCCESSFUL TOURNAMENT PLAY.

FIGURE 4.8. A THICK ROUGH CAN BE A CAUSE OF SLOW PLAY. THE PROPER ROUGH THICKNESS AND HEIGHT SHOULD BE BASED ON THE CALIBER OF GOLFER PLAYING IN THE TOURNAMENT.

irrigated roughs may not be irrigated "wall to wall"; the challenge then is to maintain the rough so that the person who just misses the fairway is not penalized more than the player who hits the shot 20 yards into the rough. This can be accomplished by using additional fertilizer and roller base sprinklers in the landing areas of the rough where the irrigation system does not reach.

FIGURE 4.9. A GOLF BALL SETTLES DEEP IN THE THICK ROUGH.

## MOWING HEIGHT AND MOWER TYPE

The mowing height for tournament play, as well as for daily play, should be a mutual decision made by the golf course superintendent, the golf professional, and a representative from the tournament committee (greens committee, owner, or board of directors). This group must discuss what the objective of the golf course is on a daily basis and how that might change during the course of the season, based on special events or tournaments scheduled. The bottom line, however, is the caliber of golfer who will be playing the course during the season. If the majority of play comes from higher-handicap players, or if the facility is a daily-fee course where the number of rounds each day is vital to the success of the golf course, the rough should be maintained at around 2 inches. If, instead, the golf course is frequented more by lower-handicap players, or is a private club, then height can be raised to one the membership is comfortable with. Consideration should be given to the type of grass used in the rough as some species lend themselves to allowing the golf ball to settle down into the turf at higher heights making the recovery shot much more difficult.

There are many good mowers to choose from for mowing roughs. On many golf courses, the option of choice is reel mowers, set up in a gang formation, based on striping and the amount of area that can be covered in short amounts of time. The problem with these mowers, however, is that when mowing roughs at 2 inches or higher, they tend to lay the grass over and do not give a clean cut. This also creates an unfair situation: the player who is in the rough and whose ball is laying in a stripe cut in the direction of play will have an easier shot than the player whose ball is in the stripe that was cut in the opposite direction of play. The point is, at the same time striping of the roughs is very pleasing to the eye, it can also have an effect on playability, especially in tournament golf. For this reason, rotary mowers are the best option for mowing roughs. A rotary mower will lift the grass blades up and cut them off clean, leaving a turf that is more upright and uniform. If production is an issue, there are rotary mowers available that can mow widths up to 16 feet.

## NATURAL VERSUS MAINTAINED ROUGH

### Natural Rough

Natural rough at many golf courses is referred to as "no-mow" areas. These may be out-of-play areas the golf course has decided to no longer maintain due to budget reasons, or an area that has been allowed to grow naturally to strengthen a hole or to create a habitat area for wildlife. Whatever the reason, natural rough should be evaluated as part of tournament preparation. Determine whether it will give one player an advantage over another, how it will affect the pace of play, and if it will cause any unnecessary rulings. Do this as part of the golf course inventory, to give you and your staff enough time to make any needed changes and have the area back in top condition before the event. Make this decision only after soliciting input from the golf professional and a representative of the tournament being hosted by the golf course.

### Maintained Rough

Maintained rough is the area just outside the intermediate cut that is mowed, fertilized, and sometimes irrigated just as all other maintained turf on the golf course. The mowing frequency is once or twice per week; the nitrogen fertilization is based on the type of grasses used, the soil conditions, and the climatic conditions, and adjusted accordingly.

Many times, as mentioned previously, when budgets are cut, golf course superintendents are forced to look for areas where they can lower maintenance requirements and, sadly, often the rough becomes the target. When this happens, the first thing that becomes noticeable is thinning density; and once stress sets in, recovery is slow, if it happens at all. To provide a level playing field for tournament competitors, the rough must be treated like the rest of the golf course, and that means providing a uniform penalty area for those players whose shots enter it from any point on the golf course.

## INTERMEDIATE ROUGH

The intermediate rough, also known as the "step cut," is the area that surrounds the fairway and, in most cases, the green. This cut should also include walkways from the teeing ground to the fairway. The width of this cut varies from golf course to golf course, but should be consistent on any single golf course. When choosing the proper width of this area for your golf course, you and anyone else involved in decision making should take into consideration the following:

- The distance from fairway bunkers to the fairway and from greenside bunkers to the green. What will adding another cut between these bunkers and the areas they protect look like, and, more importantly, play like?
- When making a pass between a bunker and a green, will there be just a thin strip of grass left (less than 1 to 2 inches) or will there be adequate separation between the greenside bunker and the green?
- Will there be too much space between the fairway bunker and the outside edge of the step cut, preventing an additional cut from meeting the architect's design intent?

Another area that needs to be examined closely is the relationship between the collar around the green and the step cut.

- Is the collar around the green smaller or larger than the step cut?

- How big are the greens? Adding a step cut around the greens essentially gives the golfer a bigger target, whereas having no step cut shrinks the target to just the actual size of the greens.

In most cases, the intermediate rough should be cut at approximately 1 inch. This will give adequate separation from the fairway height and the primary rough height. This also means that the step cut should be made in grass that will perform adequately at the 1-inch height without additional maintenance. Choose a piece of equipment that will give a high-quality cut at the 1-inch height; the width of the step cut should match up with one pass of that machine. At the same time, it may be advisable to make two passes in the walkways to give players the opportunity to walk side by side during the tournament. If the walkways are not being cut in the morning prior to play, you will want to remove the dew from the grass surface when the dew is being removed from the fairways (Figure 4.10). In areas where bunkers come in to play, set up the step cut so that if thin strips of turf are going to

FIGURE 4.10. DEW MAY NEED TO BE REMOVED FROM FAIRWAY SURFACES, TEE SURFACES, AND INTERMEDIATE CUTS PRIOR TO TOURNAMENT PLAY.

be left once the cut is made, they are cut with an additional pass by the mower. In areas where a bunker sits back away from the fairway, you'll have to decide between widening the fairway or moving the bunker closer to the fairway. I recommend discussing this issue with a golf course architect.

## OBSTRUCTIONS

When checking on the roughs as part of the golf course inventory, look for any obstructions, things such as a low branch that may impede a player from taking a backswing, or that may block a shot by a player who just missed the fairway and is in the intermediate cut but has no shot because of the low-hanging branch (Figure 4.11). This may sound like trying to make it easier for the golfer, but in fact the purpose is to remove low-hanging branches

FIGURE 4.11. IDENTIFY OBSTRUCTIONS TO REMOVE DURING THE GOLF COURSE INVENTORY.

that impede *every* player in the intermediate cut, to make the golf course fair for all competitors.

Another reason to look for obstructions is to minimize the incidence of rulings during the actual competition. This will speed up play and make for an enjoyable round of golf for everyone.

## SUMMARY

While the greens make up the area where most of the golfer's shots are played, the tees, fairways, and roughs play just as an important role in the game of golf. Great care must be taken to ensure that these turf areas are properly watered and fertilized and that the proper pesticides are used so that healthy turf can be maintained on a year-round basis. Proper cultural practices such as aeration and thatch removal are extremely important in the health of the turf plants as well. With the proper inputs and cultural practices leading to healthy turf, preparing these areas for tournament play will be much easier. The recovery period after the tournament stress is relieved will also be much shorter.

Because of the vast area that can be covered by the tees, fairways, and roughs, many of the necessary practices take a great amount of time. It is necessary that the golf course superintendent communicate what the plans are for these areas with others on the management team so that all can work together to ensure the work can be accomplished with as little disruption and inconvenience to the golfers as possible.

# CHAPTER FIVE

# BUNKERS

According to the USGA Rules of Golf, "A bunker is a hazard consisting of a prepared area of ground, often a hollow, from which turf or soil has been removed and replaced with sand or the like. Grass-covered ground bordering or within a bunker is not part of the bunker. The margin of a bunker extends vertically downward, but not upward. A ball is in a bunker when it lies in or any part of it touches the bunker." By definition, then, a bunker is not a water hazard, so you must make sure that bunkers continue to drain well. It is also important to maintain bunkers to have a firm playing surface. And, as the rule states, the bunker is meant to be a hazard, so any golfer who hits a shot into it should expect to incur a penalty stroke, unless he/she makes an excellent recovery shot. To accomplish this consistent level of playability, it is important to monitor these bunker components:

- Design elements
- Construction and drainage
- Sand selection
- Maintenance and preparation

## BUNKER DESIGN ELEMENTS

Successful playability of bunkers starts with good bunker design, which is determined primarily by three factors:

- The bunker's location in relationship to the green or fairway
- The lay of the land around the proposed bunker
- The location and elevation of the outlet site for drainage—water from surrounding surfaces must not drain into the bunker

Figure 5.1.  Basic Bunker Design.

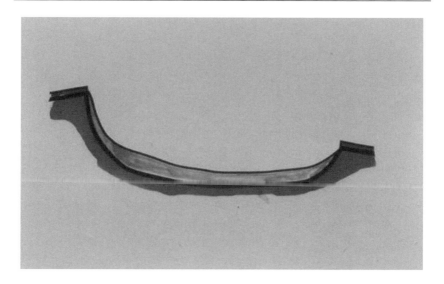

This design concept will generally yield bunkers that slope slightly from back to front, where the part of the bunker farthest away from the target is at a lower elevation than the area of the bunker nearest the target. Figures 5.1 to 5.4 show four common bunker design configurations.

Figure 5.2.  Rolling Bunker Design.

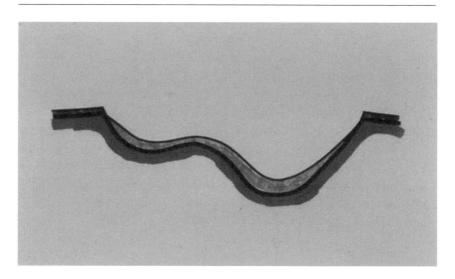

FIGURE 5.3. BACK-TO-FRONT BUNKER DESIGN.

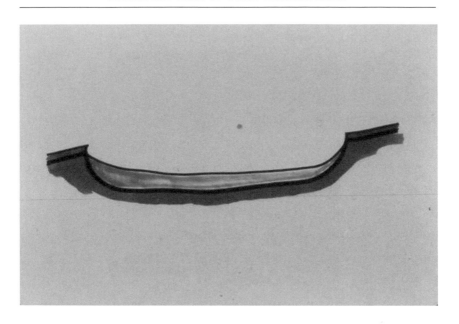

FIGURE 5.4. STEEP FACE BUNKER DESIGN.

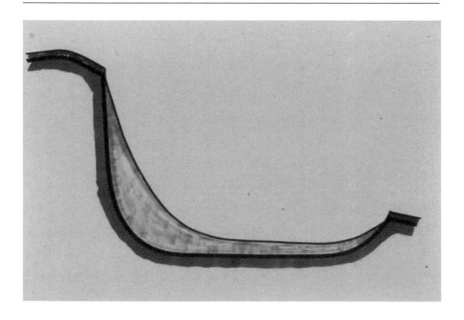

Long-term maintenance of the finished product is another critical design issue. For example, bunkers with steep faces, with sand covering those faces, often cause maintenance headaches for golf course superintendents and their staff (see Figure 5.4). On rainy days, these bunkers will wash out and need to be repaired. Therefore, if this style of bunker is desired on the course, the golf course architect will need to ascertain that the facility's budget will be able to accommodate the level of maintenance necessary to keep them in top condition. In general, most superintendents prefer bunkers that are flat on the bottom, shallow, and with grass down the face to the sand line (see Figure 5.5). These bunkers typically play well, do not wash out, and are easy to maintain.

Bunker design must also take visibility into consideration—that is, the golfer must be able to see where the hazard is.

FIGURE 5.5. SHALLOW, FLAT BUNKER.

## OTHER BUNKER DESIGN CONFIGURATIONS

There are a number of other bunker designs, all of which are acceptable as far as design is concerned, but long-term maintenance must be the determining factor to ensure the success of the bunker to the course and its players.

- *Pot bunkers*: These are small, usually round bunkers located around the green or in a cluster of fairway bunkers. These bunkers, which played a role in the history of golf, were introduced in England and subsequently made famous in the United States due to the designs of golf course architect Pete Dye.
- *Stacked sod-wall bunkers*: Another historical bunker design, stacked sod-wall bunkers have been used extensively in the United Kingdom, but much less so in the United States. They require maintenance beyond the normal required for bunker floors and for drainage; the stacked sod wall needs to be replaced about every five to seven years (see Figure 5.6).

FIGURE 5.6. STACKED SOD-WALL BUNKER.

FIGURE 5.7. WASTE BUNKER.

* *Waste bunkers*: These have become popular with golf course architects over the years, as they are an effective way to prepare a large area (some can be an acre or so) that requires little maintenance. A waste bunker (Figure 5.7) is located in an area that usually attracts only an extremely wayward shot; as such, it typically requires raking only once per day and does not need to be cut on a weekly basis, saving budget dollars.
* *Other*: Additional bunker configurations include beach bunkers, bunkers with trees located in them (Figure 5.8), and bunkers that weave through natural areas.

## CONSTRUCTION AND DRAINAGE

Following the design phase, bunker construction commences. The overall success of the performance of the bunker hinges on this stage. Specific issues to monitor include:

FIGURE 5.8.  BUNKER WITH A TREE.

- *Proper construction of the bunker floor*: This is important so that water will not become trapped between the drain tiles and, thus, create wet areas within the bunker.
- *Good outlet with a positive flow*: This is a must for draining water from the bunker.
- *Good-quality pea gravel*: This is used to cover the drain tile. It should be small enough that it will not work up through the sand and contaminate the sand, but large enough so that it cannot clog the small perforations in the drain tile, causing drainage problems in the bunker. Once the pea gravel is installed, it must be mounded up 4 to 6 inches, so that while other construction is continuing, the drain tile and surrounding gravel will not become contaminated. When the bunker is ready for sand, the excess gravel should be removed.

Figure 5.9 identifies the various areas of bunker construction.

FIGURE 5.9. BUNKER CONSTRUCTION FACTORS.

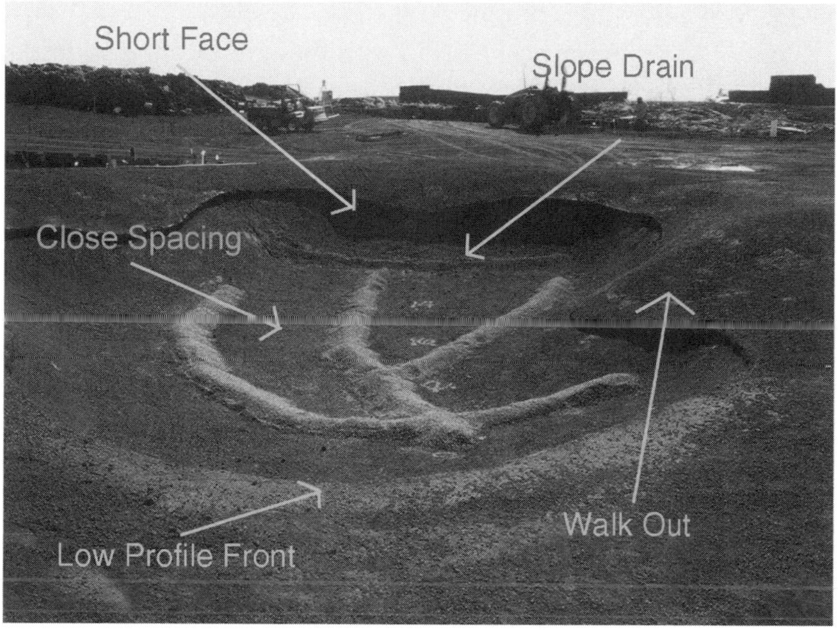

## MAINTAINING EXISTING BUNKERS

For existing bunkers with drainage problems, it is imperative to discover the cause of the poor drainage. Start by noting which bunkers on the course hold water, as well as areas within each bunker where the water is slow to drain. To address the problem, follow these steps:

1. Pump the water from the bunker.
2. Remove the sand in the area to expose the drain tile and gravel surrounds.
3. Remove the gravel around the tile and inspect it for contamination, then check the drain tile for blockage.
4. If no contamination is found in the gravel, and the drain tile perforations are not plugged, cut the tile open to continue

(*Continued*)

the investigation inside the drain tile. If there is nothing apparent when the tile is cut open, flush water through the tile to see if the tile will drain. If it does, reassemble it with a new piece of drain tile and backfill with new gravel; then add sand back to the area.

5. Observe the area during several rain events to see if the problem returns.

If during the flushing process you discover the tile will not drain, you will have to probe farther to find the blockage. There are a number of ways to do this, but the simplest is as follows:

1. Run a piece of metal wire through the tile until it encounters the blockage.
2. Use a wire tracer to follow the route of the wire through the tile to the blockage.
3. Dig up the tile, remove the blockage, and repair the tile.

In a majority of older, established bunkers, the drainage problem is usually within the bunker and is usually a contamination problem.

## ADDING DRAINAGE DURING CONSTRUCTION

When adding drainage to a bunker during construction, the most common drainage pattern is a herringbone (Figure 5.10). At the lowest point of the bunker, where the drain tile is exiting the bunker, there should be an arced tile (called a smile drain), which will allow any accumulated water to drain off. It is vital to make sure that drain tile extends into any small lobes of the bunker, to help quickly remove it during rain events. This will make it possible to quickly open the golf course for play once the rain has stopped. Note that in most cases, using the natural slope of the bunker floor to remove this water will get the job done, but not in a time-effective manner. It generally takes too long for the water to move along the floor of the bunker in search of a nearby drain tile.

FIGURE 5.10. BUNKER TILE CONFIGURATION.

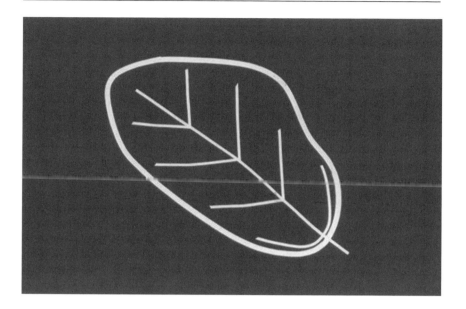

When installing tile into a bunker floor, monitor the crew doing the work to verify they are following the recommendations of
the golf course architect or the standard tile installation
instructions.

Many golf courses today are using liners to reduce maintenance costs on bunkers. Bunkers with high faces, those prone to
washing out during rain events, usually benefit the most from this
practice—if the liners are installed correctly. If the bunkers on
your course are to be lined, check that the liner is installed *below*
the perforated tile. With some of the newer liners that have come
on the market in the last few years, it is possible to line *over* the
bunker tile and still have adequate drainage; but prior to using
this method, contact the liner manufacturer for a recommendation. Figures 5.11 and 5.12 show drain installations without and
with a liner, respectively.

Two types of liners are available on the market: fiber weave
and soil sealant. Both serve their purpose, but each has its problems, which you need to be aware of before choosing the best
type for your course.

FIGURE 5.11. PROPER DRAIN INSTALLATION WITHOUT A LINER.

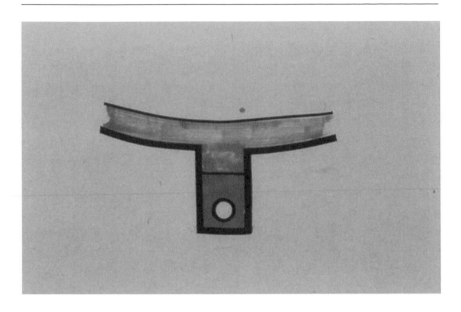

FIGURE 5.12. PROPER DRAINAGE WITH A LINER.

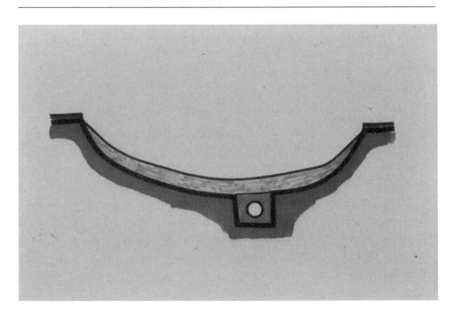

FIGURE 5.13. A BUNKER LINER THAT HAS BEEN PULLED UP
BY A MECHANICAL RAKE.

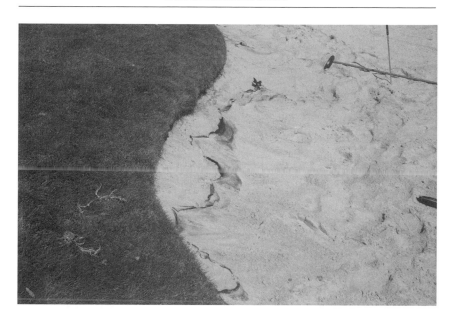

Fiber weave liners:

- May break down over time.
- Can bunch up and snag a rake or golf club face (Figure 5.13).
- Are difficult to install and repair.
- Are prone to soil blockage over drains.

Soil sealant–type of liners:

- Can erode when exposed to water.
- Are difficult to install.
- Break down under foot and maintenance wear.
- Are susceptible to fine particles plugging up sand and drain gravel.

Note that most liner manufacturers recommend adding an extra 1 to 2 inches of sand to bunker bottoms to stop the wicking action of the water in the sand, which leads to the sand surface retaining moisture and remaining wet all day.

## Sand Selection

Sand selection for most golf courses is bound by two constraints: budget and type of sand available locally. To get the best sand available for the bunkers on your course, obtain samples from local distributors and send them to a reputable USGA-approved laboratory. The laboratory will make recommendations which to choose based on: particle size distribution, probability of the sand producing "fried egg" lies, and crusting over.

Two other determining factors are sand color and shape. Many golf courses prefer white sand, but some of these can be too bright, which on a brilliant sunny day can temporarily blind a player whose ball is in the bunker. It is desirable to use sand that is angular, not rounded, as the rounded sand tends to remain loose and produce buried (fried egg) lies. In terms of shape, angular sand will set up and give a firmer playing surface and will also be somewhat resistant to washing off of steeper slopes.

Once you have identified two or three sands, it's a good idea to install each of them in a few of the bunkers—preferably in a practice area, so that the members or regular golfers can try out the sands and help the facility decide which is the best for the course. After preference has been ascertained, the next step is to present a cost analysis to course management, for the final decision on the sand that is right for the club.

With the sand chosen and arrangements made for its delivery, your next responsibility is to check batches periodically for uniformity, and to verify that the sand you are getting is the sand that was tested and used in your trial bunkers. Begin by sending a sample for every one hundred tons; if the sand continues to meet the specifications, you can reduce the frequency of sample testing. If, however, a test fails to meet the specs, reestablish the initial frequency.

Sand guidelines to keep in mind:

- In general, a majority of sand particles should be between .25 and 1.00 mm. Particles smaller than .05 mm. (silt and clay) should be kept to a minimum; and by all means, avoid particles larger than 2.00 mm.

Testing Laboratory
Certificate #13579

Page: 1 of 2

# HTML LABS

**1550 Park Place, Lawrence, Kansas  Phone: 000-000-0000**

## Report of Test Results

**Report To:** JIM JAMES
JAMES SAND & GRAVEL
**Address:** E3481 Hwy 22
Sandusky, OH 40385

**Report Date:** August 29, 2007
**Date Received:** August 10, 2007
**Test Dates:** August 16 to 29
**Condition of Sample(s):** intact

**Re:** Bunker Sands Quality Control

**Lab ID & Job Sequence:** 013672 B

## Particle Size Analysis*

| Sample # & Type | Sample Description | Soil Textural Components [Reported Values are % of the whole] | | | | | Sand Distribution by Size — Size reported as Mesh = & mm [Value Reported is % Retained] | | | | | |
|---|---|---|---|---|---|---|---|---|---|---|---|---|
| | | Sand .05-2.0 | Silt .002-.05 | Clay <.002 | #10 Gravel 2.0 mm | #18 v. Coarse 1.0 mm | #35 Coarse 0.5 mm | #60 Medium 0.25 mm | #80 Fine 0.18 mm | #100 Fine 0.15 mm | #140 v. Fine 0.10 mm | #270 v. Fine 0.05 mm |
| | USGA Recommended Specifications for Root Zone Mixes | ≥89% of Total | ≤5% ≤10% w/#140 + #270 | ≤3% ≤10% w/#140 + #270 | ≤3% ≤10% #10 + #18 | ≤10% ≤10% #10 + #18 | ≥60% #35 + #60 | ≥60% #35 + #60 | ≤20% #80 + #100 | ≤20% #80 + #100 | ≤5% #140 + #270 & ≤10% w/ Silt + Clay | ≤5% #140 + #270 & ≤10% w/ Silt + Clay |
| 1 S | bunker sand A | 98.33 | 0.75 | 0.55 | 0.37 | 3.76 | 26.84 | 53.4 | 10.55 | 1.95 | 1.26 | 0.50 |
| 2 S | bunker sand B | 98.37 | 1.07 | 0.52 | 0.04 | 0.54 | 10.99 | 64.2 | 15.39 | 3.24 | 2.69 | 1.30 |
| 3 S | bunker sand C | 98.05 | 0.68 | 0.42 | 0.85 | 7.50 | 25.22 | 46.5 | 12.54 | 3.22 | 2.30 | 0.75 |
| 4 S | bunker sand D | 98.37 | 0.83 | 0.60 | 0.20 | 2.57 | 25.49 | 54.5 | 10.60 | 2.96 | 1.69 | 0.54 |
| 5 S | bunker sand E | 98.40 | 0.86 | 0.54 | 0.20 | 9.86 | 36.21 | 43.0 | 6.70 | 1.29 | 0.84 | 0.50 |
| 6 S | bunker sand F | 98.39 | 0.97 | 0.56 | 0.08 | 1.53 | 22.28 | 61.2 | 9.76 | 1.78 | 1.22 | 0.55 |
| 7 S | bunker sand G | 98.34 | 0.77 | 0.52 | 0.37 | 3.16 | 30.29 | 50.13 | 11.15 | 3.23 | 1.10 | 0.20 |
| 8 S | bunker sand H | 91.62 | 5.15 | 0.92 | 2.31 | 13.58 | 20.70 | 34.79 | 11.92 | 4.05 | 3.63 | 2.98 |

*ASTM F1632 & C136 - Reported values are the average of two test samples

## Bunker Sand Analysis*

| Sample # & Type | Sample Description | Moisture Content - % in field - | Penetrometer Values [kg/cm²] | | | |
| --- | --- | --- | --- | --- | --- | --- |
| | | | 'Fluffed' Dry | 'Settled' Dry | 'Fluffed' Moist | 'Settled' Moist |
| 1 S | bunker sand A | 4.01 | 2.0 to 3.25 | 2.75 to 4.75 | 2.25 to 2.75 | 4.5 to >4.75 |

*NML SOP, Moisture content prediction based on -50 cm tension table

| Sample # & Type | Sample Description | Crusting | Color⁺ | | | |
| --- | --- | --- | --- | --- | --- | --- |
| | | | Munsell Color Name | Hue | Value | Chroma |
| 1 S | bunker sand A | None | Light yellowish brown | 10YR | 6 | 4 |

*NML SOP, ⁺Munsell Soil Color Chart

## Particle Shape / Size Parameters / Ksat

| Sample # & Type | Sample Description | Sphericity / Angularity* | D85* [mm] | Infiltration Rate** [in./hr. Ksat] |
| --- | --- | --- | --- | --- |
| 1 S | bunker sand A | Low to Medium to High Sphericity, Sub-Rounded to Rounded | 0.80 | 62.74 |

*ASTM F1632, **ASTM F1815

120

Figure 5.15. Proper Sand Distribution Consists of 4 to 6 Inches of Sand on Bunker Bottoms and 1 to 2 Inches of Sand on the Faces.

- Distribute sand evenly along the bunker floor, 4 to 6 inches of sand (compacted) on the bottom and 1 to 2 inches on the faces. Remember to increase the sand on the bottom of the bunker if a liner is to be used, as described earlier. Do not, however, increase the amount of sand on the face, as this raises the probability that a golf ball will get buried in the face.

## Maintenance and Preparation

Once the bunkers have been properly constructed, and the correct sand has been chosen and verified, the daily maintenance and preparation of the bunkers begins. This will encompass many practices, whose emphasis and importance will, in part, be determined by the geographical location of the golf course. But, in general, bunker maintenance and preparation will consist of the following:

- Ensuring proper sand depth
- Keeping drainage functional
- Preventing hardpan formation

- Cleaning out debris
- Defining the margin
- Raking to perfection

## ENSURE PROPER SAND DEPTH

As golfers play shots out of bunkers, and the bunkers age, they will lose some of the sand that was put in them initially. Therefore, a basic and critical responsibility of the maintenance staff will be to periodically check the depth and consistency of the sand.

For this purpose a probe can be made from an old golf club shaft or a piece of rebar that has the depths of 4 and 6 inches marked on it. This instrument can then be used to probe the bottoms of the bunkers, seeking areas that do not have enough sand, as well as those with too much sand. Too much sand comes from bunkers that wash out; when the sand is shoveled back up, commonly it is not shoveled from the area where it was deposited by the water but rather from the area nearest the washout. The result is that the area closest to the washout is very low on sand; conversely, the one farther away has too much. You can sometimes resolve this situation by moving sand around within the bunker itself, returning it to its original condition. At other times, it will be necessary to bring in new sand and add it to the bunker. Just be sure it is the same type of sand that is currently in the bunker. Note, however, that new sand of the same type may be of a slightly different color. This can be made less noticeable by using a mechanical bunker rake or a rototiller to work in the new sand with the old. And if the added sand is loose compared to that in some of the other bunkers on the course, it may be necessary to tamp or water the sand to help firm it up.

Aging bunkers will also be more prone to drainage issues from time to time. It is very important to stay on top of this. Earmark bunkers that are draining slowly, and assign a staff member to identify the drainage problem and get it corrected quickly. If it rains during the tournament, you do not want to waste time pumping out bunkers so that play can resume. During a tournament, the time right after a rainfall should be spent making sure the sand is not washed out or in need of repair instead of pumping bunkers.

## PREVENT HARDPAN FORMATION

Bunkers that have been in play for a number of months may start to form a hardpan layer just below the depth reached by rake tines. This is similar to what happens to the greens profile after aerification has been done to the same depth for many years. Sands that tend to firm up very quickly are more prone to forming the hardpan layer. It is less of a problem in looser sands, unless they become contaminated with soil.

It is important to loosen this hardpan area periodically to allow the bunkers to continue percolating water through at the same rate they did when they were established. Note that the type of sand chosen for the bunkers will play a role in how quickly hardpan becomes a problem.

The easiest way to check for a hardpan layer is to do so in conjunction with checking the depth of the sand. Instruct staff members to insert the probe slowly and feel for the hardpan as the instrument moves through the profile. Another way is to dig down into the sand with the toe of one's shoe until the hardpan is found or the excavation is below the rake-tine depth.

If hardpan is discovered, there are a number of ways to alleviate it. The easiest method is to use a mechanical rake with only the flat-blade rakes attached and with the cultivator bolts set as deep as they will go. If the mechanical rake is equipped with a cultivator attachment, this may be used as well. If it is the first time this has been attempted, the hardpan may be so thick that the bunkers may need to be gone through two or three times. With the mechanical rake in the bunker, start in the center of the bunker and go in very tight small circles; drive very slowly, and work around the bunker in these tight circles until the entire area has been covered. Then check to see if the hardpan has been removed. I warn you, this is a very slow process, so if the bunkers are being prepared for a tournament, do it months in advance; then repeat the procedure closer to tournament time (approximately six weeks), but early enough that the sand will have time to firm up on top and be ready for tournament play.

In extreme cases, where the hardpan is very thick, it may be necessary to use a small rototiller. This machine will churn up the sand, loosening and removing the hardpan layer. Just be sure that

---

**NOTE**

The spin-raking process will also help to smooth and level the sand in the bottom of the bunker, and is a good process to use for bunkers that are hand-raked daily and become wavy.

---

the sand is deep enough so that the rototiller does not penetrate the clay bottom and churn the clay into the sand, thus contaminating it.

## CLEAN OUT DEBRIS

Over time, bunkers inevitably become contaminated with grass clippings, leaves, stones, and even divots. It is necessary to clean out this debris. Especially in the fall and after storms, trees lose their leaves forming loose debris that must be cleaned out regularly so that it does not become buried in the sand or, worse, become a rules-of-golf problem.

There are many ways to clean out bunkers, depending on the type of debris you're dealing with. For debris that is light and laying on top of the sand, a simple leaf rake will do. For debris that is heavier, an aluminum bunker rake may be required. When debris is mixed in with the sand, it may be necessary to manufacture a sifting box to shovel the sand into and separate out the debris. There are also bunker rakes on the market that have screens over them, and these will work if the debris is just under the surface; they do not perform as well when the debris is throughout the entire depth of the sand. If the sand is contaminated with stones, it may be necessary to remove the sand and identify the source of the stones and then remove that source, to avoid future contamination.

## DEFINE THE MARGIN

Any time a bunker has been put in play, its edge must be defined. This is done by edging the bunker so that it is clear to the golfer whether the golf ball is inside or outside of the bunker (Figures 5.16 and 5.17). This is important because the rules of

FIGURE 5.16. EDGING A BUNKER.

golf call for the golfer to incur a penalty if the golf club is grounded while the ball is in the bunker.

There are several mechanical edgers on the market. Some are self-driven while others are hand-held; many come as attachments for weed eaters. The biggest problem with the self-driven mechanical edgers is that they do not float to stay perpendicular to the bunker face. Consequently, on steep faces, the knife on the edger may actually be underneath the edge of the bunker, cutting soil and setting up the new edge for future failure.

One of the best ways to edge a bunker is with a hand-edging tool (often, a sod knife). Using this method, pull the sand back away from the edge, 2 to 3 feet, and then edge the bunker. Remove the sod and confirm the bunker shape is established as the architect intended. Inform staff doing the edging that they do not have to remove a large amount of sod to establish a sharp edge with good turf around the entire bunker. Once the edge is

FIGURE 5.17. IS THIS GOLF BALL INSIDE OR OUTSIDE THE BUNKER?

established, examine the bunker slopes for any ridges around the area where the sod was removed. If any appear, smooth them and then replace the sand around the lip of the bunker.

Once a good edge has been established, it should be maintained periodically by using a string trimmer, both vertically and horizontally, to form a nice, clean, crisp edge. Take care that no edge is damaged when taking equipment in and out of the bunker; use a piece of plywood as a ramp for entering and exiting the bunker. If mechanical rakes are used, instruct operators to use different exit points each time the bunker is raked, to avoid mounding sand at the exit point. Also caution operators to use extra care when the mechanical rake has a blade on the front of the machine for pushing sand. This blade can come in contact with the edge of the bunker and destroy the perfect edging, making re-edging necessary.

As a bunker is used, sand may be splashed upon its face, thereby elevating the face and making it very challenging to grow healthy turf. Therefore, after a few years, examine these faces

FIGURE 5.18. THE EDGE OF THE BUNKER MAY NEED TO BE DEFINED BY A PAINT LINE, WHEN NOTHING ELSE WORKS.

with an eye to removing the excess sand and resodding the faces. In the interim, it may be necessary to sod the area next to the bunker so that a margin can be defined. In areas where sod cannot be grown, due to soil conditions or outside factors, you may have to define the margin of the bunker with turf paint (Figure 5.18). If this is done during tournament conditions, note this on the local rules sheet to help minimize rulings by officials.

## RAKE TO PERFECTION

There are many challenges to achieving perfectly raked bunkers, the biggest of which may be that it is just hard work. That is why it is essential when preparing bunkers, either for regular or tournament play, to train maintenance staff how to rake bunkers and explain why it is important to rake them that way. Consistency is another challenge. When staff set out to rake bunkers, usually they do a good job on the first few bunkers, but as time goes on and they grow tired, the quality slips, especially if the bunkers are being hand-raked.

The environment, too, can play a role in the quality of the bunkers when it comes to raking. Bunkers that tend to dry out, or are in areas that do not receive much moisture, may be difficult to rake because dry sand tends to spread away from the rake tines instead of leaving slight furrows, as it does when it is slightly wet. This problem can become long term if irrigation upgrades have led to the removal of overhead irrigation that once applied water to the bunker, and now small heads direct water to only the bunker faces. When the sand is too dry to rake, it may be necessary to add water to the bunker using the overhead irrigation system or, if necessary, by hand-watering.

### Types of Rakes

The proper rake depends on the type of sand on the golf course and so will vary with each facility. For daily maintenance, mechanical bunker rakes are a convenient way to efficiently and effectively rake the bunkers. Attachments available for mechanical rakes can produce a variety of finishes on the sand, from leaf rake attachments that leave furrows to broom attachments that leave a smooth finish. For those clubs that elect to hand-rake bunkers on a daily basis, long-handled rakes with heads similar to the ones supplied for the golfers, are advisable. These rakes will ease the wear and tear on the staff and pay off at the end of the day; bunkers at the end of the maintenance route will look and play more like the first bunkers raked that morning.

Like any other piece of equipment, rakes, both mechanical and hand, must be well cared for. Sand is very abrasive and will wear down the plastic heads on bunker rakes very quickly. Likewise, the metal end on leaf rakes will wear away quickly. It is not uncommon to use two or three sets of rake heads during a season, depending on how many bunkers are on the golf course.

If mechanical rakes are used, train operators to go slowly and stay off the faces; these must be hand-raked. If mechanical rakes are used on the faces, flat areas may form, leaving an area where a ball can become trapped, unfairly giving a golfer a very difficult shot.

In the past, for tournament play, the recommendation was to rake the bunker in the direction of play, to avoid a furrow of sand

FIGURE 5.19.  BALL IN A RAKE GROOVE.

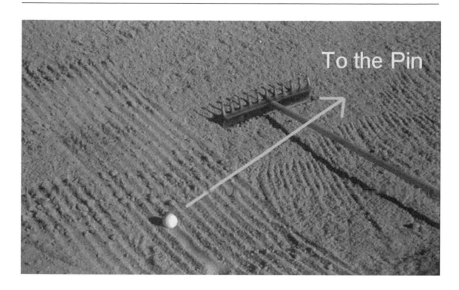

FIGURE 5.20.  PROPERLY RAKED BUNKER.

forming behind the ball, interfering with the clubface making contact with the golf ball (Figure 5.19). In fact, more important than direction is consistency; when all bunkers on the golf course are raked in the same direction, either parallel to the fairway and green or in the direction of play, no player gains an advantage over another player (Figure 5.20).

# SUMMARY

Like the turf areas, bunkers play an important part in the game of golf. While they are a hazard, they are the only maintained hazard on the golf course, thus challenging the golf course superintendent to find the balance between proper maintenance allowing for a reasonable chance for the golfer to recover and maintaining them so perfectly that the golfer would rather be in the bunker as opposed to the surrounding rough area. In order for bunkers to be properly maintained, they need to first be designed properly, then constructed properly. Once these two tasks are completed the correct sand must be chosen that will perform from a playability standpoint for the golfer and a funtionability standpoint for the golf course superintendent. This will allow the bunkers to be raked to perfection and give the appearance of hazards that are ready for tournament play.

# CHAPTER SIX

# NEAR-TERM
# TOURNAMENT
# PREPARATIONS AND
# FOLLOW-UP

Once the overall plan for the tournament has been laid out, and you and your staff have taken care of the long-term course preparations, it's time to start addressing the near-term maintenance practices leading up to the event. This chapter addresses those tasks, which include:

- Cup cutting
- Applying fertilizers and chemicals
- Conditioning the practice area
- Setting up the course and pace of play
- Marking the golf course
- Scheduling staffing and maintenance
- Managing professional tournaments

This chapter also covers post-tournament requirements:

- Doing cleanup and restoration
- Conducting a post-tournament evaluation, including a budget review

# CUP CUTTING

Cup cutting is done every day on most golf courses, yet to achieve tournament readiness, I recommend that you implement a very detailed procedure to ensure that the holes are cut properly, the flag sticks are straight, and the old cup plugs have been replaced correctly. Commonly, when cups are cut for daily play, workers are in a hurry or have other jobs to do at the same time, and they don't give the task the attention it deserves. That's why, for tournament cup cutting, I suggest that cup cutters be relieved of any other duties so that they can focus on cutting cups, and nothing else. Also, assign enough manpower to this work; you don't want employees to have to hurry in order to stay ahead of play. In terms of actual numbers, I recommend the following: if groups are starting on holes one and ten, assign two cup cutters, one starting on the first hole and the second starting on the tenth hole. If the tournament format calls for a shotgun start, it may be necessary to use four people to cut cups; if this is the case, start as early as possible in order to finish prior to start time. In this situation, a cup cutter would start on hole one and go forward, while another would start on nine and work backward. Use the same format on the back nine with the other two cup cutters.

When cutting cups, whether for tournament play or daily play, be sure to use a hole rotation to achieve balance when setting up the golf course. You can determine the hole location by a daily rotation such as front, middle, or back, or a number system for the day of the week. When choosing a system, remember it is important to produce a balanced golf course, one that does not favor one player over another. To do this, the golf course should have the same number of hole locations cut on the left side of greens as the right, and a balance of front, middle, and back locations. For daily play, and to help with the speed of play, you may want to use nine easy locations and nine medium-difficulty locations; for club tournaments or outings, the rotations may include six easy, six medium-difficult, and six difficult hole locations. Typically, for special events and tournaments, such as member-guests and club championships, a pin sheet is used that shows the location of each hole, along with the depth of the green and the

FIGURE 6.1. A TYPICAL HOLE LOCATION OR PIN SHEET USED BY MOST CLUBS AND PROFESSIONAL ORGANIZATIONS.

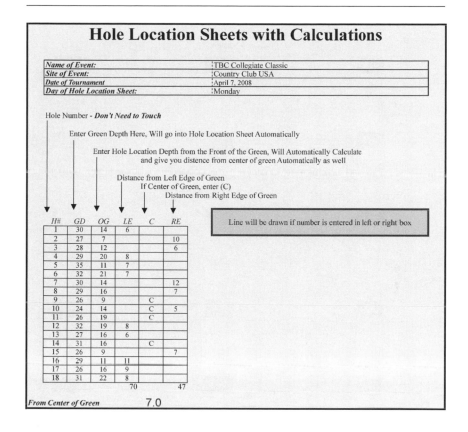

number of paces from the front and side of the hole location (see Figure 6.1).

When choosing hole locations for special events, as well as for daily play, train cup cutters to be aware of the tee locations and the wind direction each day. A few weeks prior to the event, work with the person who will be choosing hole locations for special events such as club championships or member-guests, so that the areas around these locations can be saved.

All of these techniques together will result in good hole locations that are properly cut and do not favor one golfer over another.

FIGURE 6.1. (CONTINUED)

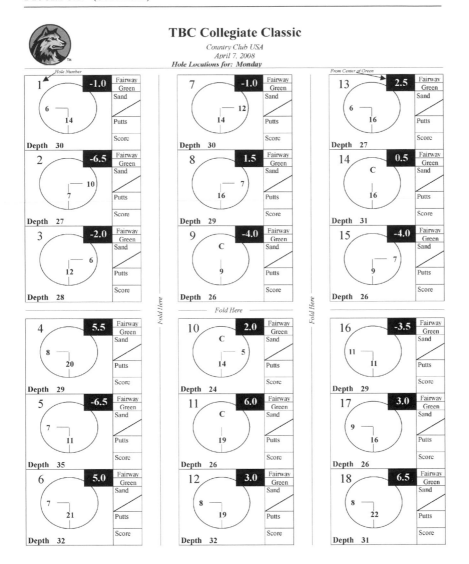

## CUP-CUTTING TOOLS

It is imperative to give cup cutters all the tools they need to do the job you have outlined in the maintenance plan for the tournament. These tools include:

FIGURE 6.2. MANY TOOLS ARE REQUIRED TO PROPERLY CHANGE PUTTING GREEN CUPS.

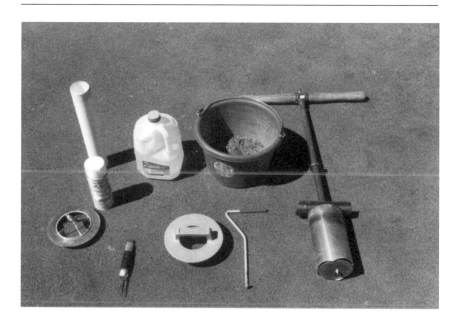

- Cup cutter
- Cup puller
- Cup setter (aluminum)
- Bucket for sand
- Water jug
- Divot repair tool (altered fork)
- Hand roller
- White paint and stencil (if tops of cups are to be painted)

## CUP CUTTERS AND PULLERS

Cup cutters and cup pullers are standard pieces of equipment. Some cup cutters will require operators to use a hammer to pound them into the green to remove the plug. This will require care, because if the operator misses with the hammer and strikes the green, at the very least the resulting damage will need to be repaired; at worst, it may render the hole location unusable. If the latter occurs, you have a real problem on your hands if pin sheets are being used and a new hole location must be chosen.

For this reason, I advise against using this particular type of cup cutter for tournament play. A cup cutter that is pushed or twisted into the green with a foot or hand eject works much better.

The blades on the cup cutters must be sharp. Dull blades lead to unsightly holes with ragged edges. Each person assigned to cutting the cups should be responsible for sharpening the cup cutter every day. This does not take much time to do, and the result is hole edges that are nice and sharp.

### Cup Setters, Buckets, and Water Jugs

The cup setter should be aluminum, to avoid getting burrs or dents, as sometimes happens on the plastic variety. As to buckets, any type can be used; the only caution is to prevent sand or greens mix from building up in the bucket so that it becomes heavy and leaves a ring mark when set on the green. It is also advisable to smooth off any lip on the bottom of the bucket that might leave a mark in the vicinity of hole locations.

Choose water jugs large enough to contain as much water as needed for the number of holes the cup cutter will change. Plastic water bottles and soda pop bottles are favorites among cup cutters because they are lightweight and easy to work with. But if plastic pop bottles are used, they must be well rinsed prior to use. Plastic one-gallon milk jugs are probably the best choice for carrying water during cup cutting.

### Optional Tools

The remaining tools on the list—divot repair tool, hand roller, and white paint and stencil—are optional, but they are helpful in producing the best-quality results when changing a cup.

Machine-made divot repair tools, which all golf shops carry, are available, but the best tool is one you can easily make by hand. Simply take a table fork and cut off an outside tine and alternating inside tine to make a long-handled divot repair tool. For comfort, you can wrap shrink tubing and duct tape around the handle. Use the tool to sew the replaced plug together once it has been inserted back into the green (Figure 6.3). Remember to check the plug for grain (this will be less important if you follow the steps in Chapter Three to minimize grain), and make sure it falls in line with the surrounding turf.

Figure 6.3. A Dinner Fork Can be Modified for Use as a Divot Repair Tool, to Sew an Old Cup Plug Back Together and Make it Less Noticeable to the Golfers.

Once the plug is back in the green, the cup cutter can take the tool and work it around the outside of the plug and then around the inside of the plug; this will raise the edges and allow them to return to an even form after the hand-roller is used to smooth the area. The hand-roller can also be used around the new hole location, if the operator pulled the edges of the new hole up when the cup cutter was removed from the green.

If the decision was made at your golf course to paint the top part of the new hole just above the line, you will need white paint. There are companies, such as Hole in White, that sell paint specifically for this purpose. If the holes will be painted by hand, practice is important so that an even amount of paint is applied all the way around the holes. Likewise, if aerosol paint will be used. The operator must get enough paint on the soil to cover it up but not so much that it drips and runs into the cup liner. You'll also need a stencil if you're using aerosol paint, which must be set properly so that the paint is distributed on the soil and does not overspray on the putting surface grass.

# APPLYING FERTILIZERS AND CHEMICALS

As tournament time approaches, the golf course superintendent is often asked about the color of the golf course, especially when the event is to be televised. It is critical that this be discussed and decided upon during the planning stages of every tournament so that a fertilization schedule can be set that will make it possible to satisfy the color demands of the committee, as well as achieve the other conditioning goals such as greens speed. It will be impossible, for example, for the golf course superintendent and staff to accommodate a demand that the golf course be made greener the week prior to, or the week of, the event.

To achieve the desired color and conditioning goals for the tournament, the first step is to find a nitrogen source that offers a high level of assurance (possibly a fertilizer product you have used before or one a trusted colleague has recommended). You may also want to avail yourself of one or more of the many nutrient and micronutrient products available, which will give good plant color without causing a flush of growth.

With the product choices made, you can start to plan the fertilization schedule that will enable you to meet the course conditioning goals set by the committee. As described earlier, the key is to have a balanced nutrition plan that allows you to maintain control of the growth of the turfgrass plant. To maintain this control, choose a method of measuring the growth of the turf in the various areas of the golf course (greens, tees, fairways, and roughs). The best way to do this is to monitor clipping yield, as discussed previously. If greens are being cut every day, you or your assistant should check the clipping yield every day to see if more or less grass is being cut than the day before. Based on the information you derive from doing this, develop a fertilizer plan that incorporates adding fertilizer as the clipping yield decreases or, conversely, adding nothing if yield is holding steady (see Table 6.1). Note: This system works best if you are applying liquid fertilizers on a weekly or biweekly basis. If a preventative fungicide program is being used, the biweekly plan fits nicely within the fungicide program.

Pay close attention to the amount of growth that results after the application of the product, and how long it is before you

TABLE 6.1. SAMPLE FERTILIZER PROGRAM FOR FAIRWAYS IN A NORTHERN
CLIMATE WITH A JUNE TOURNAMENT DATE

| Analysis and Type of Product | Application Date | Rate of Nitrogen (N) per 1000 sq. ft. |
| --- | --- | --- |
| 19-26-5 Granular | March 30 | .7 lbs N |
| 19-2-19 Granular | April 20 | .5 lbs N |
| 20-20-20 Liquid | May 10 | .2 lbs N |
| 18-3-5 Liquid | May 24 | .1 lbs N |
| 1-0-25 Liquid | June 1 | .05 lbs N |

notice a change in clipping yield (an increase and then a decrease). Of course, weather and growing conditions can be factors in these changes, and you should note these as well. In this way, you will know when to make the last application of fertilizer prior to the tournament to obtain optimum color and still meet the established conditioning goals.

On greens that are constructed from sand and fairways, and tees that are built out of or on top of sand, maintaining the desired intensity of green color can present a real challenge to the golf course superintendent. In these locations turfgrass growth may be adequate but the grass color may appear pale or faded. To solve this dilemma, consider adding iron and other micronutrients such as manganese, which may add color to the turfgrass plant without contributing much growth. As recommended throughout this book, experiment first with any untried micronutrient products; you want to know in advance, and record for future reference, the length of time the greening effect will last.

Don't neglect the periodic soil and tissue tests, as discussed in Chapter Two. At the same time it is important to work toward satisfying the needs of the plant. You must also plan any needed applications around scheduled preparation for important tournaments. If the applications must be made during a time of the year when the tournament will be held, you must consider the consequences of the application (increased plant growth, etc.) and make allowances in the fertilization program prior to the tournament to achieve the conditioning goals for the event.

The planning process for chemical applications is much the same as it is for fertilization, and will be initially determined by the instructions you're given by the tournament committee regarding conditioning goals for the event, in conjunction with any budget restrictions. And the chemical application schedule you draw up will be determined in part by the time of year the tournament is to take place. You'll have to account for any pests that may pose a threat to accomplishing the conditioning goals set. If, say, the tournament is scheduled for a time of year when a particular disease or insect outbreak is possible, or even probable, your objective will be to make a chemical application as close as possible to the tournament date (usually the Friday prior); the goal is to avoid applying chemicals during the event.

When preparing to use any pesticide, the first step is always to read and follow the instructions on the label—the label is the law. The next step is to properly train the staff who will be applying the pesticides; they must fully understand the consequences of making a mistake. For example, the effects caused by an overlap of a preemergent herbicide may not be apparent for up to six weeks, which could run right up against the date of the tournament. Thus, you, as golf course superintendent, must carefully plan each application so that the maximum benefit can be realized at the minimum risk. Record each application and note any irregularities (Table 6.2). This will give you critical information should an area of turf start to look bad for no apparent reason.

TABLE 6.2. SAMPLE CHEMICAL APPLICATION RECORD*

| Chemical Name | Application Date | Rate | Irrigation | Rainfall | Comments |
|---|---|---|---|---|---|
| Merit | May 15 | .15 oz/1000 sq ft | 1/2 inch | 0 inches | Not watered in on hole 15; rough, irrigation leak |
| Subdue Max | July 1 | 1 oz/1000 sq ft | 0 inches | 1 inch | Rainfall occurred two hours after application |

*These applications are a minimum; the more detailed the record, the more helpful it will be in the future.

FIGURE 6.4. THE OHIO STATE UNIVERSITY DEVELOPED THIS CHEMICAL FAMILY CHART TO HELP SUPERINTENDENTS CHOOSE CHEMICAL COMPOUNDS THAT REDUCE THE POTENTIAL FOR DEVELOPING RESISTANCE.

**Families of Fungicides for Turfgrass**     1/2008

THE OHIO STATE UNIVERSITY EXTENSION

J. W. Rimelspach, T. E. Hicks & M. J. Boehm, The Ohio State University, Department of Plant Pathology

| Common Name | FRAC Code[2] | Trade Names[1] | Mode of Action | Placement/ Mobility | Concern Over Resistance | Comments |
|---|---|---|---|---|---|---|
| **Chemical Family: Dithiocarbamates** | | | | | | |
| Mancozeb | M3 | Fore, Mancozeb, Dithane T/O, Protect T/O | general | contact | low | These types of fungicides have broad-spectrum control properties and are used as protectants. Early development of these started in the 1930's. |
| Thiram | M3 | Spotrete, Defiant, Thiram | | | | |
| **Chemical Family: Dicarboximides** | | | | | | |
| Iprodione | 2 | Chipco 26GT, Raven | specific | local penetrant | moderate to high (not persistant) | The dicarboximides were developed in the mid-1970's. These fungicides have broad-spectrum activity. |
| | | Iprodione Pro, 18 Plus | | | | |
| Vinclozolin | 2 | Touché, Curalan | | | | |
| **Chemical Family: Benzimidazoles** | | | | | | |
| Thiophanate-methyl | 1 | Cleary's 3336, T methyl Pro, T-Storm | specific | systemic (upward) | high | This family of fungicides became available in the late 1960's and ushered in the era of systemic fungicides. The development of resistance to the benzimidazoles is a serious problem. |
| **Chemical Family: Sterol Inhibitors or Demethylase Inhibitors** | | | | | | |
| Fenarimol | 3 | Rubigan | specific | systemic (upward) | high | This group of fungicides was introduced in the late 1970's and has broad-spectrum activity. At times, referred to as the SI's or DMI's. The development of resistance to this family of fungicides is a serious problem. |
| Myclobutanil | 3 | Eagle | | | | |
| Triademefon | 3 | Bayleton, Accost | | | | |
| Propiconazole | 3 | Banner MAXX, Spectator, ProPensity, Kestrol, ProPimax | | | | |
| Triticonazole | 3 | Trinity | | | | |
| Metconazole | 3 | Tourney | | | | |
| **Chemical Family: Strobilurins** | | | | | | |
| Azoxystrobin | 11 | Heritage | specific | systemic (upward) | high | First product available in 1997. The chemical structures are found in various naturally-occuring, wood-decaying fungi. Broad spectrum disease management chemical tools. |
| Trifloxystrobin | 11 | Compass | specific | local penetrant | high | |
| Pyraclostrobin | 11 | Insignia | specific | local penetrant | high | |
| Fluoxastrobin | 11 | Disarm | specific | systemic (upward) | high | |
| **Chemical Family: Carboxamides or Anilides** | | | | | | |
| Flutolanil | 7 | ProStar | specific | systemic (upward) | low | The first family of successful systemic fungicides to hit the market in 1966. With the exception of Emerald, carboxamide fungicides are highly effective against Rhizoctonia and other basidiomycetes. |
| Boscalid | 7 | Emerald | specific | systemic (upward) | moderate to high | |
| **Additional Fungicides... each is in a different chemical family** | | | | | | |
| Chlorothalonil | M5 | Daconil, Manicure, Pegasus, Echo | general | contact | low | Listed are other important fungicides. Some give broad spectrum control. Since these compounds represent different chemical groups, they are placed together here. Chlorothalonil is a protectant fungicide. PCNB is usually considered to be a protectant but may be locally systemic. |
| PCNB | 14 | Terraclor, Turfcide, Revere, FFII, PCNB, Defend, Engage | general | contact | low | |
| Fludioxonil | 12 | Medallion | specific | contact | low to moderate | |
| Polyoxin D zinc salt | 19 | Endorse | specific | local penetrant | moderate | |
| **Oomycete (Pythium) Fungicides ... in different chemical families** | | | | | | |
| Mefenoxam | 4 | Subdue MAXX, Apron (seed treatment with Metalaxyl) | specific | systemic (upward) | high | Few diseases besides those caused by Pythium species and yellow tuft, are controlled. Azoxystrobin (Heritage) and Pyraclostrobin (Insignia) are unique with activity against both Pythium species (Oomycetes) and the fungi. Fosetyl-aluminum is a true systemic exhibiting both upward and downward movement in plants. It is also unique in that it moves in the phloem (symplastic transport) as compared to all other systemic fungicides that are transported in the xylem (apoplastic transport). |
| Propamocarb | 28 | Banol | not well known | systemic (upward) | low | |
| Pyraclostrobin | 11 | Insignia | specific | local penetrant | high | |
| Fosetyl-Aluminum | 33 | Prodigy, Chipco Signature, Autograph | not well known | systemic (up & down) | low | |
| Azoxystrobin | 11 | Heritage | specific | systemic (upward) | moderate to high | |
| Chloroneb | 14 | Teremec SP | general | contact (local penetrant) | low | |
| Ethazole (Etridiazole) | 14 | Koban, Terrazole, Truban | general | contact | low | |
| Cyazofamid | 21 | Segway | specific | local penetrant | moderate to high | |
| phosphite (salts of phosphorous acid) | 33 | Magellan, Biophos, Resyst, Alude, Vital | general | systemic (up & down) | low | |

[1]Product list by trade name may not be all inclusive.
[2]FRAC codes indicate the biochemical target site of action, according to the Fungicide Resistance Action Committee. M3 and M5 indicate multi-site inhibitor, with no significant risk of resistance.

141

FIGURE 6.4. (*CONTINUED*)

# Products that contain more than one fungicide:

| Product Name: | Active Ingredients: |
|---|---|
| Armada | triadimefon + trifloxystrobin |
| Concert | propiconazole + chlorothalonil |
| ConSyst, Spectro, Peregrine | thiophanate-methyl + chlorothalonil |
| Headway | azoxystrobin + propiconazole |
| Instrata | propiconazole + chlorothalonil + fludioxonil |
| Junction | copper hydroxide + mancozeb |
| LESCO Twosome | fenarimol + chlorothalonil |
| MANhandle | myclobutanil + mancozeb |
| Prostar Plus | triadimefon + flutolanil |
| Proturf Fluid Fungicide, Dovetail | iprodione + thiophanate-methyl |
| Proturf Fluid Fungicide II | metalaxyl + triadimefon |
| Proturf Fluid Fungicide III | triadimefon + thiram |
| Proturf Fungicide IX | thiophanate-methyl + chloroneb |
| Tartan | triadimefon + trifloxystrobin + stress guard |
| Systar | thiophanate-methyl + flutolanil |
| 26/36 Fungicide | iprodione + thiophanate-methyl |

# FRAC - Fungicide Resistance Action Committee

**FRAC is a Specialist Technical Group of CropLife International**
(Formerly Global Crop Protection Federation, GCPF).

The purpose of FRAC is to provide fungicide resistance management guidelines to prolong the effectiveness of "at risk" fungicides and to limit crop losses should resistance occur.

**The main aims of FRAC are to:**

1. Identify existing and potential resistance problems.

2. Collate information and distribute it to those involved with fungicide research, distribution, registration and use.

3. Provide guidelines and advice on the use of fungicides to reduce the risk of resistance developing, and to manage it should it occur.

4. Recommend procedures for use in fungicide resistance studies.

5. Stimulate open liaison and collaboration with universities, government agencies, advisors, extension workers, distributors and users of products.

**FRAC Code:** Numbers and letters are used to distinguish the fungicide groups according to their cross resistance behavior. The numbers were assigned according to the time of product introduction to the market. The letters refer to P = host defense inducers, M = multisite inhibitors, and U = unknown mode of action and unknown resistance risk.

For more information go to -   **http://www.frac.info/frac/menu.htm**

So far, I've mentioned weather only briefly, in passing, but now I want to address it more fully, and the impact it can have on your tournament planning. As the days count down to the event day, begin paying close attention to long-range forecasts that cover the days of the tournament. The rule of thumb here is that if predicted conditions raise concerns, the time to apply a preventative spray would be the week prior to the event, as most pesticides (especially fungicides) will give at least seven days of control under moderate to heavy pressure. Ideally, you will have been keeping a record of any chemical resistance problems that have occurred in the past on your course, which you can now use as a guide to choosing a product in a chemical family that has not shown this characteristic. The Ohio State University has developed a chart to help you make this choice (see Figure 6.4).

If the forecast is for an extremely dry period during the tournament, and there are areas on the golf course—especially the greens—that are notorious for drying out, you may opt to apply a wetting agent on these areas, to try and minimize any hand-watering that would need to be done during tournament time. Once again, work closely with the staff members who will be applying the wetting agent to make sure they understand the importance of getting the product watered in thoroughly after application, to avoid potential burning of the leaf surface. The best way to apply wetting agents on greens is via hand-watering using wetting agent tablets. This allows direct application of the wetting agent to the areas that need it without affecting other areas that don't.

## CONDITIONING THE PRACTICE AREA

Keeping practice areas in top condition can be a real challenge for a golf course superintendent and the maintenance staff at any time of the year, but with a tournament date on the near horizon, this area will see increased use due to the number of players now intensifying their efforts to improve their game. The objective, of course, is to condition the practice area so that it plays the same as the golf course, to give players an accurate gauge of how they'll be hitting shots from the fairway, or chipping and putting on the green. The challenge is to accomplish this pretournament conditioning while these areas are still being used for daily play.

## PRACTICE FACILITIES AT OLDER GOLF COURSES

Key to maintaining a well-conditioned practice facility is to have enough space so that you can move around the hitting areas to accommodate the amount of play, as well as provide recovery time for areas that have just been used. This is more problematic for practice facilities (especially range tees) at older clubs that have not been renovated. They were not built to handle the amount of play they receive, and thus it is a constant struggle for the superintendent to maintain healthy turf in these areas. It is not uncommon for golf courses built in the last 10 years to have one and half to two acres of range tee. Many clubs have even resorted to using dual-ended range tees to ensure there is enough teeing area for their players for the entire season.

Similarly, with the more recent advances made in the design of golf clubs and golf balls, coupled with the increasing ability of today's golfer, depth is also becoming a problem on older ranges, forcing many golf courses to erect netting along the sides, and especially at the ends of the driving range, to accommodate the golfers.

## MAINTAINING RANGE TEES

To maintain a healthy range tee, the maintenance staff will have to follow a regular schedule of topdressing and fertilization, which you, the superintendent, have established as part of your long-term planning. To accommodate these practices, it may be necessary to close the range tee for a short period of time, one or two days per week. (As noted in Chapter One, it's a good idea to communicate the importance of closing the range tee to the players via a newsletter or postings in the clubhouse.) Choose less busy times for this, such as early in the morning on less active days at the tee. Keep in mind that even with a good topdressing and fertilization program, it will take approximately 21 to 30 days for a used area of range tee to recover fully and be ready for activity again during a tournament.

Logically, the size of the area tournament players need will depend on the number of participants, as well as the type of event. For example, a shotgun-start tournament will require a larger teeing area than an event using a tee-time start. If the event is a full field event (144 players), ideally, there should be enough room for all of the players to practice at the same time. For professional tournaments this is especially important, since the participants will be practicing before their tee time and after their round is complete. Therefore, 30 days prior to the tournament you may have to block off the section of range tee that will be used during the tournament so that it will be in the proper condition for tournament play. If the tournament will extend over several days, save enough area to accommodate the number of players who will be on the course each day. And if multiple events are scheduled within a short time frame, and the course must accommodate daily play at the same time, you, in cooperation with the tournament committee, will need to decide in advance how to handle the range tee situation. If the range tee cannot handle the events as well as daily play, the only option may be to use mats for daily play during the periods between events so that turf recovery is possible for the event after the tournament of focus (e.g., member-guest followed by a club championship).

During the tournament, the range tee should be cleared of any divots, and the area used during that day topdressed. The teeing area should start at either the front of the tee and work back each day, or at the back of the tee and work forward each day. There are two schools of thought on this process. One says that, for recovery purposes, it is best to start at the back and work forward, so that as the area is cleared of divots, the new sand and seed are not blown away, if debris blowers are used. The second focuses on the participants and preventing them from walking over an area that has been topdressed. Thus, if the hitting areas are moved back each day, the participants will be walking on good turf as they enter the practice area. Either option is acceptable; use the one that best fits your course, equipment, and personnel.

The cutting height of the range tee for tournament play should be the same as that on the fairways that will be played during the event. Likewise, on practice greens and chipping greens, the pace should be the same as that set for the tournament. This is very important, so that the players can get a feel for how the golf course will be playing before they ever set foot on the course. When this practice is not followed, players may view it as "tricking up" the golf course.

The best time for mowing the range tee during tournaments is in the morning prior to use. If this cannot be done, make arrangements for the dew to be dragged from the tee surface before it is used. For the putting green, it may also be necessary to cut extra holes to accommodate the number of players who may be using it prior to play. If you're preparing for a multiple-day tournament, change the putting green hole locations every day to avoid wear and damage to the practice putting green. This can be done the evening before, to ease the burden on the maintenance staff. Change the other holes on the tournament greens on the day of the tournament, after the green has been mowed. This will prevent damage to the hole during the mowing operation, which would force you to abandon the hole location and find a new one.

## NOTE

During practice rounds for professional events, it may be necessary to find space for club repair and club sales personnel who might be traveling with the professional golfers. These do not have to be large areas, but they do need to be in close proximity to where the players are practicing. Also, place buckets of water on the range tee, for club cleaning. And speaking of water, players appreciate it when drinking water is provided within easy access of the range tee.

# SETTING UP THE COURSE AND PACE OF PLAY

Many factors are involved when it comes to addressing pace-of-play issues at golf courses around the world. You, in coordination with the maintenance department, can improve the pace of play in a number of ways. Probably the easiest is to communicate on a daily basis with the golf professional, to stay informed of any special events or special groups that might be playing at the facility. Set up regularly scheduled meetings for this purpose, or discuss this information during the weekly staff meeting. Include in these talks any special starts, such as back nine starts, one and ten tee starts, or shotgun starts; also cover the caliber of golfers each group is bringing to the golf course.

With that information in hand, share it with your maintenance staff and begin laying out the setup procedure. Don't overlook the weather as you do this. The direction and speed of the wind can make a huge difference in the way the golf course plays; similarly, rainy or dry weather will make a difference in how long or short the golf course plays. Instruct the staff members who will be doing course setup to pay close attention to the location of each hole, especially par threes, and set the tee locations accordingly. Not only will this help produce a consistent length on the golf course, it will also help with the pace of play.

Setup personnel must also understand some of the philosophies of the golf course architect. For example, if the golf course has four par threes, setup staff should make sure that none of them plays the same length. This will help ensure that the golfer needs to hit four different clubs on the par threes during the round of golf. If the same thing can be done with the par fives, this too will present an added challenge to the golfer. It is usually rewarding for the golfers when one of the par fives is reachable in two shots by a majority of the players. For tournament play, if the reachable par five happens to be the first hole, the tournament committee may need to make a decision between playing the hole as long as possible, to limit the number of golfers who can reach the green in two shots, and shortening the hole and playing it as a par four. Choosing one of these options can be instrumental in establishing the pace of tournament play, by helping to adhere to scheduled start times. (Note that if you choose to lengthen the hole, you should make an attempt to have one of the remaining par fives be reachable in two shots.)

## MARKING THE GOLF COURSE

One of the first questions that must be answered early in tournament planning is: Who will mark the golf course? If it will be someone from your facility, this person must have a solid working knowledge of the rules of golf; they will need to know when to use a ball drop, and where it should be located; how a hazard should be marked; and what is designated by a red line, a yellow line, and a white line. Workshops are offered both in marking the golf course and the rules of golf by the USGA (United States Golf Association) and the GCSAA (Golf Course Superintendents Association of America).

The maintenance department should be responsible for supplying all stakes and paint for marking the golf course. Enough yellow, red, and white stakes should be kept on hand so that if any are damaged or removed, a new one can be put into place in short order. A supply of these three paint colors should also be on hand, for daily as well as tournament play. It's also a good idea to stock up on a few cans of green paint, for "erasing" marking mistakes, as well as a few cans of a fifth color, should anything else on the golf course need to be marked.

If the group holding the tournament is a professional or amateur golf group, they will probably assign one of their committee members to mark the golf course. You should work with this person to ensure that all of the hazards are marked and that any supplies that may be needed are readily available. For professional golf events, a lead rules official may be assigned to the site. This person will be an expert on the rules of golf and will mark the golf course well in advance of the tournament (usually the week prior). The person will probably go over the golf course two to three times, to ensure the paint lasts through the event and that nothing is missed.

### NOTE

If your golf course is marked by one of these experts, this is an opportunity to improve the reputation of your course. Continue to use those expertly made marks, to let the patrons of your facility know that the golf course has been properly marked, as well as to reduce the potential for controversy.

Regardless who marks the course, as superintendent, you are responsible for informing all concerned if there are any areas that need to be played as "Ground Under Repair." This then should be noted on the local rules sheet so that every golfer knows how to proceed if their ball comes to rest in one of these areas.

## PREPARING THE COURSE FOR MARKING

Whether you and your maintenance staff or a golf official will mark the course, you and your staff should prepare it for the marking process to speed up this important process. Trim creek and pond banks and any tree branches or tall grass from line-of-sight near out-of-bounds markers. A ball is ruled either out of bounds or inbounds by placing a string from one out of bounds marker to another out-of-bounds marker; therefore, brush and tall grass need to be trimmed so this task can be accomplished quickly and without any disputes. But once the lines have been painted, instruct the maintenance staff not to trim or mow over any of the lines until after completion of the tournament.

For professional tournaments with galleries, draw up a detailed plan of signage, roping, and staking of the golf course. All these items should be covered in the early planning meetings (six months to one year prior to the tournament) then discussed at length with the maintenance staff. Thereafter, work out the details: Who will provide the signs? When will they be delivered? Who will install them? Who will put up the rope and stakes? Who will purchase/pay for the rope and stakes?

# SCHEDULING STAFFING AND MAINTENANCE

In general, staffing a golf course for tournaments is no different from the process you follow for everyday operations: Identify the number of tasks that must be accomplished, the time necessary to complete each task, and the number of staff members required to accomplish them in the time allotted. The only difference is that you may need to institute split shifts, as during tournament time it may not be possible to complete every maintenance task prior to the round, meaning it will have to be done "after hours" to prepare the course for play the next day.

Another tournament-specific staffing objective is to identify staff members who excel at certain important jobs, such as cutting cups, mowing greens, or raking bunkers, and then assign those employees to those tasks. This will put you and the golf course in the best possible position for success. For consistency, I also advise that you have the same person or persons change the hole locations every day during the tournament. If two or more cup cutters are used, make sure they communicate with each other about the hole locations they will use on the par threes, to make sure all these holes play a different length. It's also imperative that they inform each other about the hole locations they intend to cut, so that there will be a balance of front, middle, and back, and easy, medium, and difficult hole locations. It is also nice to balance left and right hole locations, if possible.

The most difficult type of tournament to staff for is one with a shotgun start, which requires that every maintenance function be completed prior to start time, on every hole, at the same time. Often for this type of tournament you will have to alter the staff's start time to give them more time on the golf course to accomplish their tasks. And for tournaments that have a one and ten tee start, the staff must be split in half so that all maintenance tasks can be accomplished on both nines at the same time (all holes do not, however, need to be ready by the start of the tournament).

## MANAGING PROFESSIONAL TOURNAMENTS

As noted previously, the planning process for professional tournaments should start a year or more in advance—even if the golf course is only being considered as the host for the event. If your facility is chosen as the site for the tournament, time will go by very quickly, especially if it is the first such event held there.

An early must-do is to develop an overall site map. As course superintendent, you should work with the golf course architect (if possible) to produce this document, which should cover the layout of the golf course and all the land owned by the facility. From that, you will draw a more detailed map that will locate everything that will be placed on the golf course, from emergency services, public restrooms, food service, and signage to entrances, exits, and shuttle pick-up and drop-off sites. The map will be a dynamic, working document, which will be filled in as the planning process unfolds, and adjusted to accommodate changes over time. Thus it will become an important aid in making early decisions regarding tents, vendors, and sponsors—in particular, vendors that must be lined up far in advance to supply the items needed, and to schedule setup of skyboxes and tents (Figures 6.5 and 6.6).

Although these aspects of the setup process are not the direct responsibility of the golf course superintendent, you will be involved indirectly with many of the processes as they relate to the preparation of the golf course. For example, each time an item is added to the map, you should field-verify that item immediately with a member of the tournament planning committee. If something does not fit, such as a hospitality area or the media

FIGURE 6.5. TOURNAMENTS SELL SKYBOXES SUCH AS THIS ONE TO SPONSORS TO HELP RAISE MONEY FOR THE TOURNAMENT; IN RETURN, THE SPONSORS ENTERTAIN IMPORTANT CLIENTS.

FIGURE 6.6. HOSPITALITY AREAS CAN TAKE UP MANY ACRES ON THE GOLF COURSE, AND SO REQUIRE CAREFUL PLANNING.

compound, everyone involved has to be informed as soon as possible so that there is adequate time to relocate it to an area that can accommodate it. Certainly, the maintenance staff must be kept in the loop here, especially the irrigation technician, who will be monitoring the setup process to prevent damage to the irrigation system, specifically irrigation lines near areas where tents will be located and stakes will be driven into the ground.

Once the master map is finalized, make and distribute copies to everyone involved with the tournament preparations. Consider producing the final version in a computer program such as Auto-Cad, to ease the update process (see Figure 6.7).

A major area of concern for professional tournaments is spectator traffic flow. The site map can be used to identify, thus control, cart paths, spectator walkways, and other areas of movement. With those areas clearly drawn, it then becomes possible to arrive at a plan for roping off spectator traffic areas, player areas,

Figure 6.7. Computer Programs Such as AutoCad Can be Used to Produce On-Site Maps That Can be Quickly Updated for Future Tournaments.

hospitality and food vendor areas, and media accommodations. With this map in hand, travel to these areas looking for "pinch points," where traffic will back up; then go back to the drawing board to see if there is a better way to keep the traffic flowing smoothly. Sometimes, there will be no alternative, in which case, special training of the marshals working the congested area will be necessary. During this tour of the spectator paths, keep an eye out for any hazards that may lead to a spectator being injured, such as a loose board on a bridge or cracked or damaged cart path sections. Have those danger zones repaired very quickly, to prevent an injury. Likewise, check trees around spectator areas for broken or damaged limbs that could fall and injure someone passing underneath. Because these hazards may require an outside contractor to address, waste no time in booking the appropriate firm.

## HANDLING THE MEDIA

Any golf tournament may attract media, but the chances are greater of this happening when the event is a professional golf tournament. The position you should take as golf course superintendent is a proactive one. Three guidelines apply here: don't be afraid of them, make yourself available, and work with them as friends.

Weeks prior to the event, contact local media personalities who will be covering the event and introduce yourself, both to break the ice and to establish yourself as a course contact who is willing to work with them to give them an accurate account of the event's activities. If you are uncomfortable in this role, you may want to consider attending a seminar on working with the media and/or on public speaking.

## MAINTAINING MEDIA RELATIONS

If possible, stay in touch with the media throughout the year. This will ease your relations during future events. It's also an effective way of diffusing any negative interaction on the golf course or during the event. Media representatives will be more likely to contact you as their source for information. In this way, you can help ensure that an accurate story is told, one that will protect the golf course and facility employees, including yourself.

Whenever you talk to the media, state the facts, and only the facts, as you understand them; never guess at an answer. It is perfectly acceptable to say you don't know, or you are unsure of something. And keep in mind the media is often restricted to short sound bytes, so keep your responses brief and to the point. It's also a good idea to "show and tell" when possible; if, for example, you are explaining a task that is performed on the golf course, describe briefly what's happening, then demonstrate. Remember, not everyone speaks golf course maintenance talk.

As important to dealing with the media directly is preparing for their arrival. Simply put, they will need space, lots of space. For professional events, you will need to designate an area as the media compound, an area in the neighborhood of 2 acres, centrally located. Their equipment will require wires and cables that run over much of the golf course. You must inform them where they can and cannot drive carts and install their equipment. If the tournament is an annual event, it is wise to look for ways to minimize the amount of cable that needs to be laid out each year. Work with the media company to install as much of this as possible underground. This will save time and unnecessary damage to the golf course in the upcoming years.

Setting up for television coverage is a particular challenge. Television camera towers will need to be erected at key locations, and it is important that the staff erecting these structures and setting up the cameras know how to reach the site with as little disruption as possible (see Figure 6.8). If rain is in the forecast, or it has been particularly wet prior to the media's arrival, make sure to inform them and to take extra precautions. You may need to

FIGURE 6.8. TELEVISION TOWERS SUCH AS THE ONE BELOW MAY BE ERECTED BEHIND MANY GREENS AND TEES TO PROVIDE TELEVISION COVERAGE.

supply them with sheets of plywood to work from in order to minimize the damage to the course.

---

## BEHIND THE SCENES

Media representatives will be looking for stories behind the scenes, in addition to the obvious subjects of interest—the players and the event itself. You and/or the maintenance staff may be one of those stories. Should this be the case, it may be difficult for you and members of the staff to meet with the media, due to the fact that you will all be working during the event. To circumvent this dilemma, make yourself known to the person who is coordinating with the media to arrange for a mutually convenient meeting time and place.

It's also important to establish yourself as the source of current event information. If, for example, bad weather is expected and everyone is scrabbling to find what workarounds will be put in place, it is best that the media get it straight from the person responsible for making those decisions—you, the golf course superintendent.

---

# Doing Cleanup and Restoration

The inevitable final stage in hosting a tournament is cleanup and restoration of the golf course. The question you must ask first is: How much must be done immediately upon conclusion of the event? The answer is twofold, based on the type of facility and the type of tournament. If the event was a club tournament, such as a member-guest or a club championship, chances are there will not be much cleanup required. If, on the other hand, the event was a professional tournament, the opposite will be the case. As to how much needs to be done immediately depends on the facility itself and what the plans are for it the next day. If the facility is a private club, which will be closed the day after the event, you can put off most of the work until then. But if the course is a daily-fee facility, with high demand for the next day, obviously some work will have to be done so that the maintenance crew can get to work preparing the golf course for the day's play, after which they'll return to doing post-tournament cleaning and restoration.

The second question is: What type of cleanup will be needed? Here, the answer lies in the type of event. For most member-guest and club championships, cleanup will comprise nothing more than gathering a few extra coolers from the golf course and, possibly, breaking down a tent or two and adding topdressing in areas where contests may have been held.

Cleanup for professional events involves much more.

- All of the hospitality tents and skyboxes must be dismantled and removed.
- All of the ropes and staking must be removed. Most signage put up for the tournament will have to be taken down and stored. Some signs, however, typically sponsor attribution signs, may need to be left up for a period of time. This will have been predetermined by agreements the club made with these sponsors, to give them extended recognition in exchange for the time and money they donated to make the event a success. Consult with the tournament director for instructions in this area.
- All freestanding trash receptacles set out for the event will need to be collected and stored.
- Any signage or yardage posts that were removed temporarily to accommodate event-specific marking will need to be replaced prior to daily play.
- Any borrowed equipment will need to be returned to the company or golf course that loaned it for the event.

Whether a lot or a little will need to be done to restore the golf course or club to its normal operations, the cleanup phase is an important issue to cover during the planning stages for the tournament. You, as golf course superintendent, want clear directions and a thorough understanding of what needs to be done, and when, so you can pass that information on to the staff who will be doing the work. In the case of professional tournaments, this may mean communicating with outside staff, those who erected the skyboxes, put up rope and stakes for gallery control, and set up media connections. Post-tournament, they must be informed of any functions the following day that might impede their progress in removing their materials. In many cases, these professional firms will be in a hurry, to move on to the next tournament site, so you must work very closely with them to help them remove their materials in a timely manner without disrupting play or damaging the golf course.

## CONDUCTING A POST-TOURNAMENT EVALUATION

The tournament is over and the golf course has been restored to its normal operations. Yet one more job needs to be done, and it is as important as the pretournament planning. The post-tournament evaluation will bring closure to the event as well as set the stage for the next event. For this evaluation to be productive, everyone involved with the tournament must be included—you, of course, the entire tournament committee, the golf professional, and club management. All of you should meet to discuss everything that took place during the tournament. This meeting should take place within a week of the event so that all of the facts, activities, and problems remain clear in the minds of all concerned. Beforehand, however, each participant should ask those involved in the tournament under his or her direct management a series of agreed-upon review questions regarding the tournament. The answers to these questions will then become the basis of the post-tournament evaluation agenda.

As the golf course superintendent, you will be responsible for representing the maintenance staff, so in preparation for this meeting solicit their input regarding their experiences leading up to, during, and following the event. Ask what went right and what went wrong; and encourage them to make suggestions as to how things might be improved for the next event. Employees should feel free to speak their minds as they relate their experiences during the tournament; without honesty, you cannot gain a true picture of the event from their point of view. Remember, those who work in the trenches can offer a unique and highly valuable insight, and often can offer the best solutions to any problems. Take careful notes when you talk with each of these people, to take with you to the evaluation meeting.

Finally, following the meeting, keep careful records of the evaluation, in particular problems and their potential solutions, as background for preparing for the next tournament. And whenever the opportunity presents itself during regular course operations, institute the solutions to see if they might work; if not, you have time to come up with another answer. Over time, you'll be amazed and rewarded to discover how the improvements you and your staff make will be noticed by those who play in these events, as well as those involved in running them.

## REVIEWING THE BUDGET

There's no better time to review the budget than following a tournament. I've discussed earlier in the book the importance of including tournament expenses as a line item in golf course/club budgets, regardless of the type of event.

For starters, this protects you, the golf course superintendent, from changes that typically take place in club management and affect the budget and, subsequently, your ability to do your job. At private clubs, for example, it's not uncommon for the board of directors to change from year to year; the person who was the tournament chairman is now on another committee, and the new chairman wants the member-guest event to be bigger and better than ever, and likewise wants the golf course to be perfect, at whatever the cost. If there is no line item in the budget for tournament expenses, the new director might look at the maintenance budget and see no problem with spending more money to meet his/her stated objectives. You, on the other hand, have already allocated that money for certain projects, an expected number of staff, and a certain quantity of chemicals and fertilizer, and know there's nothing extra to meet the demands of the new tournament chairman. With a tournament line item in place, however, you can explain to the chairman what special things are normally done for tournaments with those dollars, then discuss other ideas the chairman has and assign cost amounts to those ideas. The chairman can then take this information to the board of directors and ask for an increase in the tournament line item, and explain the request. This method serves to buffer you—at the end of the year, when everyone has forgotten how nice the tournament was, you will not be called on to explain why you went over the maintenance budget to produce that success.

The tournament line item is, in fact, composed of a number of items:

- Extra labor hours and any benefits associated with those hours
- The cost of rental equipment
- Outside contractors
- Additional supplies, such as fertilizer for an extra application (possibly in the roughs); ropes and stakes; paint for identifying hazard markers
- Anything else tournament-specific that would incur an extra expense

Note that I did not include extra chemicals as an item in the list. That is because adequate chemicals should be purchased from the operating budget every year in order for the club to meet the expectations of its golfers.

When it comes to hosting professional tournaments, almost without exception you'll find the biggest increase in expenses to be in labor. Employees will be called on to work a tremendous number of hours to put the golf course in tournament-ready condition. Unfortunately, many clubs underestimate this expense and consequently are shocked when the payroll sheets come in after the event. Most of the hourly employees will make more in overtime pay during these periods than what they make in a typical workweek. It is not unusual for employees to work in excess of 110 hours per week leading up to and through the tournament. Therefore, it is very important to let everyone involved in the planning process, especially the finance committee, know what to expect in terms of labor requirements when hosting a tournament, especially one of professional status. This is your area of expertise, and so it is your responsibility to make this information known. More, it is critical to the ongoing success of the tournaments your club will be hosting and, ultimately, your own professional success, as well.

# IN CONCLUSION

There are many daily routines that happen on the golf course. Staff members are trained to do their jobs and sometimes many other jobs. If they only perform one of the duties they are trained for, they become very good at it, but they become rusty at those other tasks for which they are trained. As tournament time approaches, the golf course superintendent must evaluate the staff so that those who perform certain tasks very well are placed in those positions during tournament preparation. This will allow the staff to perform at its maximum efficiency during the tournament and produce a golf course that not only meets the expectations of those playing in the tournament but exceeds them. In Appendix A, you will find a Pretournament Checklist that will assist in tournament preparations. You can modify this list so that it will best suit your needs. Use this list as you plan your tournament and seek advice from the management team and tournament committee as you fill in the blanks. If this checklist is filled out approximately 6 weeks before the golf tournament you are planning for, it will become your game plan for executing flawless tournament preparation. Also in the Appendix are some course conditioning guidelines that will help you put the checklist together and better understand the thought behind some of the checklist items.

Tournament preparation is very demanding of a golf course superintendent and of a maintenance staff. Some of the information presented in this book seems very basic, but it is included here because these are the things I have seen first-hand that fall through the cracks in tournament preparation. These are little things, if corrected prior to the event, no one notices, but if they are left undone, they can become the topics of conversations after the tournament is over. You are now ready to prepare your golf course for any tournament that might come your way. Communicate well and often, plan and practice every detail to the letter, learn from this tournament to make the next one better, but most importantly, enjoy the moment!

# PRETOURNAMENT CHECKLIST

## TOURNAMENT PREPARATION CHECKLIST

Event: _____

Site: _____

Event Date: _____

People Present: _____

Visit Date: _____

### ARCHITECTURAL AND LANDSCAPE CHANGES

1. Describe any architectural changes that were made or are anticipated in the coming year.

   _____

   _____

   _____

   _____

2. Describe any course changes, such as fairway recontouring.

   _____

   _____

   _____

   _____

3. Describe landscaping changes, such as new tree plantings.

   _____

   _____

   _____

   _____

## GREENS

1. The target Stimpmeter reading for the beginning of Advance Week is between _____ and _____ feet, with the objective of reaching a reading between _____ and _____ feet during Tournament Week. To help meet these targets and produce a firm, true putting surface, the following maintenance procedures were discussed:

   - Height of cut: _____ inch
   - Fertilization: _____
   - Topdressing: _____
   - Verticutting: _____
   - Grooming: _____
   - Brushing: _____
   - Rolling: _____

2. Have at least one USGA Stimpmeter available. *Note*: It is also recommend that you have two moisture sensors, made by Turf-Tec International, and one Lang Penetrometer. (See Guidelines, later in the Appendix, for ordering information.)
3. Avoid using tournament hole locations beginning at least two weeks prior to the tournament. *Note*: All high and low cup plugs need to be repaired prior to Advance Week. Ball marks need to be repaired daily, two weeks prior to and through Advance Week.
4. (Additional Comments) _____
   _____
   _____
   _____

## APPROACHES

1. In general, cut approaches at fairway height, not rough height.
2. (Additional Comments) _____
   _____
   _____
   _____

## PRACTICE GREEN

1. Rotate a total of _____ holes daily on the practice green to accommodate the Players during Tournament Week. (*Note*: To save time during daily course setup, the practice holes can be rotated in late evening with the approval of the Rules Staff.)
2. Mow the practice green first in the rotations prior to play each morning; ensure the Stimpmeter reading matches that of the competition greens.
3. (Additional Comments) _____

_____

## GREEN COLLARS

1. Avoid high rough cut immediately adjacent to collar.
2. Height of cut: _____ inch
3. Minimum width: _____ inches
4. (Additional Comments) _____

_____

## TEES

1. Height of cut: _____ inch
2. Avoid using tournament tee areas *one month* in advance of the tournament to ensure well-conditioned tees during Tournament Week.
3. To protect par three and short par fours during Advance Week and practice rounds, cover tournament tees with plastic mesh.
4. Do any leveling required _____
5. (Additional Comments) _____

_____

## PRACTICE FACILITY

1. Close tournament tee and chipping areas _____ weeks in advance to ensure complete turf coverage.
2. Mow teeing area daily prior to play at same height as fairways *not at tee height.*
3. (Additional Comments) _____

_____

## FAIRWAYS

1. Establish mowing height of _____ inch well before the event to avoid scalped areas during the tournament.
2. Be prepared to remove dew from fairways and approaches first thing in the morning.
3. Establish fairway widths and contours as requested. Note any changes to be made. _____

   _____

4. Fill divots with a dark-colored soil mix well in advance and during the event. Avoid straight sand.
5. (Additional Comments) _____

   _____

   _____

   _____

## ROUGH

1. Height at start of Advance Week: _____ inches with a goal of _____ inches for the event. (*Note:* Be prepared to cut all rough inside ropes throughout the tournament. Rotary mowing is recommended and may be required to achieve desired height.)
2. At least one month before Advance Week, put an intermediate rough in place around the fairways of _____ inches in width and _____ inch in height.
3. Establish an intermediate rough around the green of _____ inches wide.
4. One month before Advance Week, establish walkways from tees to fairways of _____ inches wide.
5. (Additional Comments) _____

   _____

   _____

   _____

## IRRIGATION

1. Gauge irrigation applications well in advance to provide firm, fast surfaces during the event.
2. Coordinate all irrigation for Advance Week and Tournament Week with the Rules Staff.

3. Use surfactants to improve infiltration and uniformity, especially in landing areas and greens. The brand name to be used is _____.

4. Be prepared to hand-water if needed, especially greens and landing areas.

5. (Additional Comments) _____

_____

_____

_____

## BUNKERS

1. Be prepared to do additional work on bunkers during Advance Week, if requested.

2. In preparation for the event, check the sand depth in several bunkers prior to Advance Week. Where necessary, adjust the sand depth to 4 to 5 inches on bunker floors and, if practical, 1 to 2 inches on faces. Add new sand in the bunkers as soon as possible to ensure compaction and firmness. Recheck the sand depth in all bunkers Advance Week, and adjust if necessary.

3. Remove any stones or roots, and correct any other problems in and under the sand.

4. Grass or otherwise permanently outline the edges of the bunkers to enable a clear definition of limits of the hazard.

5. Establish a clean, visible edge of at least 1 inch deep on the green-side face at least two weeks before the tournament. Thereafter, lightly trim the edge by cutting. There should be only enough of a lip on opposite sides of these green-side bunkers and on all of the fairway bunkers for definition.

6. Gain approval for all maintenance and on-course rakes from the Agronomist. This will be discussed in more detail during the Agronomist's visits. Brand name of rakes to be used is_____.

7. Train staff in proper rake placement. Generally, place on-course rakes outside bunkers, in line with play.

8. Mow inside grass bunker faces as directed by Agronomist, at_____ inches in height; mow outside grass bunker faces at _____ inches.

9. Keep machine-raked bunkers free of tire tracks and ridges. Raking will be done by _____.
10. If sand is too soft, use _____ to firm up bunkers during Advance Week.
11. (Additional Comments) _____

_____


## ON-COURSE TRAFFIC RESTRICTIONS

1. To preserve the condition of the fairway landing areas and adjacent rough, limit play to 150 rounds/day during Advance Week, Sunday through Thursday; close the course Friday, Saturday, and Sunday leading up to Tournament Week. Also, restrict cart traffic to paths prior to Advance Week, and/or divert cart traffic with appropriate mobile barriers as early as possible.
2. (Additional Comments) _____

_____

_____


## RAIN PREPARATION

1. Have _____ rubber-roller-based squeegees on hand and in good repair.
2. Have at least _____ trash pumps available to remove water from bunkers.
3. (Additional Comments) _____

_____

_____

_____


## TREES

1. Remove any stakes and support wires in playing areas and spectator areas.
2. Level to grade any tree basins in playing areas.
3. Trim any low-overhanging branches and shrubs that could interfere with spectator flow, player walk paths, or ball flight.

## Cup Liners, Flagpoles, and Flags

1. *Approved* metal cup liners and flagpoles are required. Do not use plastic liners or inserts. Verify that cup liners are in good condition, so flag will stand straight. Have all new liners approved by the Agronomist or Advance Rules Official and place them in use during Advance Week to ensure easy removal of the flagpole. Flagpoles are to be white or yellow fiberglass, 8 feet in length, uniform in width (not greater than 3/4 inch, and no taper). *Flagpole and cup brand must match.*

2. When purchasing cup liners and flagpoles, follow these important guidelines:

| *Metal Cup* | | *8-Foot White Flagpole* | |
|---|---|---|---|
| *Brand* | *Part Number* | *Phone Number* | *Part Number* |
| Standard Golf Co. (www.standardgolf.com) | #18303 | 800.553.1707 | #26998 |
| Bayco (www.baycogolf.com) | #252AL | 877.668.4653 | #300W-8 |
| Par Aide White Tour Package | #TR900 | 888.893.2433 | #TR900 |

3. To paint the edges of the holes during the event, have sufficient Hole-in-White paint and two applicator devices on hand.

4. To ensure a crisp edge around the holes during the event, have an approved cup cutter on hand and in good condition.

5. Properly train the cup cutter staff in cup cutting procedures. Allow time for a cup-changing clinic during the tour Agronomist's pretournament visit. Be prepared to set up the course beginning with both the number 1 and 10 Tees. You will need two people and two sets of the recommended tools and supplies, as follows:

   - Hole cutter (new blade sharpened on the inside)
   - Tool bucket and large towel
   - Depth-setting ring (measure actual depth set)
   - Cup removal tool

- Tool to knit edges of replaced plug
- A piece of 3-inch, 1-foot-long PVC pipe (bevel sharp edges of the pipe)
- Small bottle of water
- Extra greensmix
- A small foam "brush" to remove runs of paint from the cup
- A pair of small, delicate scissors
- Hole-In-White paint and applicator, along with some method to shield painting process from the wind

6. Instruct staff to change holes only after the green has been mowed, during the actual competition.
7. Make preparations to sharpen hole-cutting equipment daily.
8. Stockpile a minimum of 27 bright yellow flags (plus one extra set).

## COURSE MARKING

1. To avoid confusion during the event, discontinue normal painting of hazards and ground under repair at least *one month* before Advance Week.
2. To aid course marking during Advance Week, remove all plant materials that impede line-of-sight between out-of-bounds stakes one week prior to the tournament. Also, as directed by Advance Week Rules Officials, trim tall grass and remove clippings and debris between hazard stakes so marking paint will adhere to the ground.
3. It is imperative to have on hand by Monday of Advance Week the following marking supplies:

- _____ cases of approved red paint (The Agronomist will designate the brand required for the event.)
- _____ cases of approved yellow paint
- _____ cases of approved white paint
- _____ cases of approved natural green paint
- Four long-handled paint guns
- Supply stakes for marking the hazards (Plastic, color composite stakes, with spike attached, 2 inches by 2 inches and 2 feet long are recommended. If the type of stake on hand has been previously approved by a Rules Official, it can be used instead.

A supply of 50 yellow and 200 red are usually enough to start with, but be prepared to be able to quickly provide additional stakes if requested.)

- Supply stakes for marking the out-of-bounds (These should be white, 2 inches by 2 inches and 3 to 4 feet long, or others preapproved by a Rules Official. Have at least **120** stakes on hand, but be prepared to quickly provide additional out-of-bounds stakes if needed.)

## EQUIPMENT

| Type | Number of Units/ Type in Inventory | Number of Items Needed |
|---|---|---|
| Greens Mowers | | |
| Green Collars Mowers | | |
| Greens Rollers | | |
| Tee Mowers | | |
| Practice Tee Mower | | |
| Approach Mower | | |
| Fairway Mower | | |
| Rough Mower | | |
| Fairway and Rough Blower | | |
| Bunker Rakes | | |
| Transportation | | |
| Auxiliary Lighting | | |

# TENTATIVE WORK SCHEDULES

| *Task* | *A.M.* | *P.M.* |
|---|---|---|
| Dew Removal | | |
| Greens Mowing | | |
| Green Collar Mowing | | |
| Greens Rolling | | |
| Tee Mowing | | |
| Fairway Mowing | | |
| Approach Mowing | | |
| Walk Path Mowing | | |
| Intermediate Rough Mowing | | |
| Primary Rough Mowing | | |
| Practice Tee Mowing | | |
| Bunker Raking | | |
| Divot Repair | | |

## STIMPMETER READINGS
### ADVANCE WEEK

DATE _____

| HOLE | PG | | | | |
|------|------|------|------|------|------|
| Monday | | | | | |
| Tuesday | | | | | |
| Wednesday | | | | | |
| Thursday | | | | | |
| Friday | | | | | |
| Saturday | | | | | |
| Sunday | | | | | |

Weather notes and anomalies: _____

_____

_____

_____

_____

_____

_____

_____

_____

## STIMPMETER READINGS
## TOURNAMENT WEEK

DATE _____

HOLE          PG      _____   _____   _____   _____

Monday        _____   _____   _____   _____   _____

Tuesday       _____   _____   _____   _____   _____

Wednesday    _____   _____   _____   _____   _____

Thursday      _____   _____   _____   _____   _____

Friday        _____   _____   _____   _____   _____

Saturday      _____   _____   _____   _____   _____

Sunday        _____   _____   _____   _____   _____

Weather notes and anomalies: _____

_____

_____

_____

_____

_____

_____

_____

_____

# COURSE CONDITIONING GUIDELINES

The purpose of the Conditioning Guidelines is to assist the golf course Superintendent and the tournament organization in achieving the goal of providing a golf course that fairly tests the Players' skill and produces fair and consistent playing conditions in all areas.

These guidelines are not directly applicable to all courses, due to differences in grass types, course design, and timing of the tournament relative to seasonal weather and turf growth. Therefore, an Agronomist may be contacted to visit the golf course in advance of the tournament. In doing so, he will work with the Superintendent, club officials, and host organization to help interpret these guidelines and make them applicable to this event. An Agronomist can outline the specifications for tournament conditioning during these visits, including green speed, fairway widths, cutting heights, and bunker preparations. He will also outline any necessary tree trimming, tee leveling, mowing contour changes, and specific irrigation practices, and review the general agronomic programming leading up to the tournament. Any requests for tee leveling and changes in mowing contours should be completed well in advance of the tournament, as determined by the Agronomist and Golf Course Superintendent.

All golfers enjoy and benefit from playing under ideal playing conditions. It is therefore recommended that the golf course be maintained as close as reasonably possible to tournament standards during the months and weeks leading up to the event. Some modifications to this may be necessary due to seasonal changes in turf conditioning requirements. The goal should be to peak the course during the week of the event, matching the requested specifications as nearly as possible without causing damage to the turfgrass.

# Greens

In general, most Superintendents will be asked to provide consistent green speeds in the range of 9-1/2 to 11 feet, as measured by a USGA Stimpmeter, by the end of Advance Week. This allows the Rules Official to make a final determination on a tournament speed, which can be adjusted up or down as required. Arbitrary and excessive green speeds can eliminate prime hole locations for the tournament, and this must be avoided. The Stimpmeter will be used frequently prior to and during the tournament to check the overall pace and consistency of all greens. It is essential that the prescribed green speed be maintained as consistently as possible throughout Tournament Week. Situations where the green speed dramatically increases or decreases as the tournament progresses must be avoided.

Firm, but not overly hard greens are the goal for tournament play. This may require hand-watering prior to and during the event. Key staff members should be trained to recognize areas of the greens that dry out and require supplemental irrigation. The use of two TurfTec Moisture Meters and, possibly, a Lang Penetrometer can assist the staff in determining how much water to apply. If conditions are extremely dry, it will probably be necessary to do some overhead watering with the automatic system during Tournament Week. This will help maintain a consistent baseline of moisture in the root zone. The TurfTec Moisture Meters are available from John Mascaro at Turf-Tec International, at 800-258-7477; the Lang Penetrometer is available from Boots Lang, at 251-968-7266.

Overwatering of greens should be avoided at all costs, as this will increase spike marks and footprints, reduce the skill required to hold a shot, and possibly cause green-side bunker sand to become overly wet. The use of a hose-end canister containing a wetting agent has proven effective in maintaining uniform moisture levels when hand-watering is required. Also, a general application of wetting agent, either through spraying or irrigation injection methods, will promote more even infiltration and reduce dew or frost formation.

Great care should be taken to keep green approaches firm during periods of irrigation. This may require shutting off the fairway approach heads so as to not add to that which comes off the green. It can be helpful to include green approaches in the regular topdressing schedule to improve surface drying. Under no circumstances should an approach be watered to the point where it is made softer than the green surface.

Frequent light topdressing may be applied right up to the start of Advance Week. This will promote improved ball roll and reduced spike marks if done as part of a regular topdressing program.

Supplemental rolling may or may not be recommended leading up to and through the tournament. It is always good to have one or two units available, however, should rolling be necessary, especially to smooth the surface after a heavy rain or Pro-Am event. If triplex mowers are used for cutting, rolling will more likely be needed.

Multidirectional greens mowing in the weeks leading up to the tournament is designed to reduce grain. Grain orientation tends to be mostly in an east-to-west direction or on downhill slopes. Therefore, it is recommended that verticutting and turf grooming take place in a true north/south direction or across the general slope of the green. This should result in more of the grass blades being cut. Drag brushing or hand-brushing should be done against the prevailing grain, which can be found by hand-brushing in a circle in a typical area of the green. Once the direction of grain on each green has been determined and marked, all brushing should be done in the opposite direction. Backtrack or reverse mowing on the same path to provide a double cut should also be done, with the first cut made against the prevailing grain direction. In preparation for the tournament and during the event, at least four mowing directions should be used: a true north/south and a true east/west, northeast/southwest, and northwest/southeast.

The following additional guidelines will help produce quality tournament surfaces:

- Use vertical mowing and grooming equipment regularly to reduce surface grain throughout the year.
- Complete all core aeration procedures to reduce thatch and compaction at least eight weeks before the tournament. Be

sure to apply enough topdressing as often as necessary to completely fill holes to the top.

- Schedule fertilizer applications so that clipping removal rates are moderate. Usually, a rate of between one-fourth and one-half basket per green is optimal one week before the tournament. The use of foliar fertilizer at light rates is recommended, starting eight weeks out, for better growth control.
- Review the previous year's hole locations or the likely selections by the Tournament Rules Officials and avoid these areas for regular play at least two weeks before the tournament.
- Ensure that all green-side sprinkler heads, drainage catch basins, valve boxes- and snap-valve couplings are leveled to existing grade to prevent being marked as "ground under repair."
- Make sure that at least eight single-unit or four triplex greens mowers are on hand, properly serviced, and set up to mow between .150 and .100 inch. Mowing heights on both cool- and warm-season grasses will vary according to the pace desired for the tournament. Walk mowers are preferred over triplex mowers for producing tournament putting surfaces.
- Have two experienced cup changers and necessary equipment on hand for the tournament. This includes a watering jug, soft brush, large towel, 3-inch PVC pipe section for hand-rolling, knitting tool, depth-setting tool, cup removal tool, extra greensmix, a pair of small scissors, Hole-in-White paint and applicator, small foam brush, and smooth-bottomed bucket to carry them in. Smooth, rubber-soled shoes and sharp cup-cutter blades are required.
- Generally, set collar or fringe width to 30 inches, unless otherwise dictated by the golf course design. Height should be between 1/4 and 1/2 inch.
- Repair all scalped or low plugs regularly, as needed, one month prior to and through Advance Week, and use extreme care in cup cutting Advance Week.

## TEEING GROUNDS

Firm, level, and closely mown tee surfaces are required for tournament play. The mowing height should be between 1/4 and 1/2 inch, depending on grass type and time of year. A major problem with many championship tees and forward tees is thatch accumulation, mainly due to lack of use. Where thatch is a problem, vigorous vertical mowing, hollow-tine aeration, topdressing, and close monitoring of fertilizer applications should occur throughout the year to eliminate sponginess. If necessary, one heavy topdressing, two to three weeks prior to Advance Week, will help ensure a firm tee surface.

Tournament teeing areas on par three and short par four holes where iron shots are played during the tournament should be closed for regular play well in advance of the event, and extra efforts should be made to fill and seed divots on a regular basis. During practice rounds, these tees may need to be protected with plastic mesh or some other suitable screening material so that undisturbed areas are available for use during the tournament.

Mowing patterns that extend past the flat portions of the tee decks or point toward the center of the landing area should be corrected.

# FAIRWAYS

Most well-designed golf courses have fairways that have various widths, to accommodate different skill levels and to enable players to approach certain pin positions on the putting surface. With this in mind, the main requirement is that fairway widths in the professional's landing areas should be in the range of 25 to 30 yards wide. There are exceptions to this, of course. Bunkers, trees, and water hazards can make it difficult to meet this standard. Narrowing fairways to a point where fairway bunkers end up set too far into the rough, or to where a prime fairway approach area is lost, will usually be avoided.

As with the greens, overwatering the fairways during the tournament must not occur. Providing a firm, uniform fairway surface over 18 holes can be accomplished if the Superintendent selectively irrigates only those fairway areas needing water for turf survival. Superintendents and irrigation technicians should practice programming their irrigation systems to achieve these conditions well before Advance Week. During Tournament Week, all irrigation to the golf course must be discussed with the Rules Officials on a daily basis.

Mowing heights in the range of 7/16 to 1/2 inch are usually specified, depending on conditions. The trend toward lightweight mowing has generally produced improved playing surfaces but can raise the potential for increased thatch development. Soft, puffy fairways should be avoided, for the health of the turf and for playability considerations. When thatch is a problem, vertical mowing, aeration, and sometimes topdressing should occur throughout the year, and be finished in time for complete healing of the turfgrass before the tournament begins.

Lightweight mowing units do allow for more frequent cross-mowing of fairways throughout the growing season, and this practice is encouraged. This reduces grain and allows surface depressions to be mowed more cleanly. Varying the mowing pattern—left to right/right to left, cross-mowing, and straight mowing—before and during the tournament is recommended. Repetitive tee-to-green mowing, to "burn in" a striping pattern, may negatively affect playability and is not encouraged. Daily mowing should begin Advance Week, including the weekend before the tournament.

Fairway settlement, including sunken irrigation or drain lines, should be repaired as part of the regular maintenance program. Many Superintendents maintain the white lines put down to designate "Ground Under Repair" well after the tournament until the areas can be properly addressed. It is very discouraging for Rules Officials to have to mark the same areas year after year on a tournament golf course, and this trend should be avoided by making the necessary repairs beforehand.

# Rough

Mowing heights for roughs are usually in the range of 2 to 4 inches, depending on the type of tournament, difficulty of the course, turf species (Bermuda is shorter), and overall density. Every effort must be made to provide a consistent rough quality throughout the entire golf course and particularly through the playing corridor. This may require selective fertilization, supplemental irrigation, and interseeding to improve turf density. Since there is a tendency for rough near the fairway to become denser because of the overlapping of fairway irrigation and fertilizing, it is important that shots hit deeper into the rough are not penalized less than those that just miss the fairway. In most cases, the normal intermediate cut at 1 to 1-1/2 inches will compensate for the potential inequity. Players prefer not to have a narrow strip of primary rough between fairway or green bunkers and the short cut turf. Thus, unless directed otherwise, extend the intermediate rough to the bunker edge in those cases. This, along with rough mowing heights and cart traffic controls to reduce wear, will be discussed more specifically during the Agronomist visits.

As the rough height is increased for tournament play, it may be to the facility's benefit to continue with the normal rough height around the teeing grounds through the beginning of the fairways. Doing this will help higher-handicap golfers and likely speed up Pro-Am rounds.

# BUNKERS

In an effort to maintain tournament bunker conditions, adhere to the following specifications:

- Install all major inputs of new sand far enough in advance of the tournament to ensure compaction and firmness.
- Through frequent probing, ensure there is a uniform settled depth of 4 to 5 inches throughout the bunker floor. If steep faces are part of the design, these areas should have no more than 2 inches of sand, to prevent buried lies. If this is not possible, the sand must be firm enough to prevent balls from plugging into the slope. When sand is redistributed to maintain consistent depths, or after heavy rains, make sure all areas are properly settled. Tamping, rolling, and/or hand-watering to firm these areas may be necessary, as long as it does not require excessive effort and time, to the detriment of other preparations.
- When mechanical bunker rakes are used on a regular basis it can result in a tendency for the sand to "fluff," or become overly soft. When this occurs, remove cultivator bars and protruding spikes from the machines, or at least shorten them, prior to the tournament. When requested, begin hand-raking of bunkers two weeks before the tournament. Avoid extreme ridges, troughs, or waves during Tournament Week. The use

of hand brooms or brush attachments may also be requested to help firm the surface of soft sand where significant potential exists for buried lies.

- In some instances, mechanical cultivation may be necessary to loosen overly compacted sand in bunker bottoms, to achieve the requested performance standards for the competition. This is usually done in the evening by "spin" raking with cultivation attachments, followed by a light hand or mechanical raking in the morning to provide the proper "finish" to the surface.
- Always hand-rake small bunkers, and make extra efforts to maintain consistent sand depths. Large bunkers may be raked mechanically, if necessary, with fan rakes or other suitable smoothing devices attached to the rake bar. Check all mechanical rake exit points for excessive sand depth and proper edge contouring.
- Complete edging of bunkers one month before the tournament. Thereafter, hand-trim the grass runners, as needed.
- Green-side grass bunker slopes may be requested to be mowed, to prevent hanging lies. In other circumstances, due to design considerations, the bunker slopes may be mowed at primary rough height. The Agronomist will discuss this with the Superintendent during one of his visits prior to the tournament.
- Remove all stones, roots, and debris regularly throughout the year. Final stone removal must be completed prior to Advance Week, and monitored daily thereafter.
- Before purchasing new sand for replacement or capping, send several samples from local sand suppliers to a USGA-approved physical soil testing laboratory for a Bunker Sand Suitability Analysis. These labs can predict the playing quality of the sand and recommend the best choice for tournament play. While ideal sand may not be available in all areas of the country, every effort should be made to find the best possible material for your region. Color should be a secondary consideration to performance.
- For sand to drain quickly over a given period of time (a minimum of 20 inches per hour), and to minimize damage to the surface of a putting green or to the mowers, it should have the following characteristics:

- A minimum of 65 percent of the sand should be between 1 mm and .25 mm. Of the total sand, no more than 25 percent should be .25 mm or smaller. No more than 5 percent of the total sand should be .15 mm and smaller.
- The combination of silt and clay should not exceed 3 percent of the total sample being considered.

A penetrometer reading, to determine the degree a given sand will resist buried lies, can be obtained from a USGA-accredited lab, along with the particle size distribution and water infiltration rate. However, the penetrometer test has a wide degree of variability from lab to lab, so it is critical that you check the performance of any given sand prior to mass installation. It is also preferable that the sand particles have some degree of angularity so that fine and very fine particle content can be kept to a minimum.

Not all regions of the country have affordable and available sand that meets ideal performance criteria. Nevertheless, it is vitally important to work with an accredited testing laboratory to help select the best sand possible for the situation.

## PLAY RESTRICTIONS

It is recommended that all play be restricted to no more than 150 rounds per day during Advance Week, Sunday through Thursday, with the course closing on Friday, Saturday, and Sunday leading up to Tournament Week. This will allow the greens, tees, and landing areas time for recovery from divots, ball marks, and wear, as well as provide nondisruptive work time for tournament preparation. If Sunday is used for tournament purposes, the course closing should begin on Thursday. In addition, restricting cart traffic to paths prior to Advance Week and/or diverting cart traffic with appropriate mobile barriers as early as possible would be very helpful.

## COURSE MARKING

Professional-level competitions require that the golf course be thoroughly and properly marked. This will be done by the Rules Official during Advance Week. In preparation for marking, address the following, as requested:

- Supply stakes for marking the hazards. Plastic, color-composite stakes with a spike attached, 2 inches by 2 inches and 2 feet long, are recommended. However, if the type of stake on hand has been previously approved by a Rules Official, it can be used instead. At the start of Advance Week, have on hand an adequate number of stakes, based on previous tournament experience or as requested by the Rules Official.
- Supply stakes for marking the out-of-bounds. These should be white stakes, 2 inches by 2 inches and 3 to 4 feet long, or others preapproved by the Rules Official. At the start of advance week have on hand an adequate number of stakes, based on previous tournament experience or as requested by the Rules Official.
- Stock the following: 2-pound mallet, 10 cases of red paint, 3 cases of yellow paint, 3 cases of white paint, 1 case of natural or forest green (not florescent) paint, 1 case of blue paint, and 4 matching paint guns. The Agronomist will designate which brand of paint is requested for the event.
- Mow a swath completely around all hazards and lateral hazards. This swath needs to be about 20 inches wide and about 1 inch high. Unless otherwise indicated by the Advance Rules Official, mow this swath about 2 feet away from the edge of the water, unless the bank is too steep to permit this; in that case, mow the swath as close as possible. Clear all grass clippings and debris from the swath, to ensure that a clean paint line can be applied.
- Mow between each out-of-bounds stake to permit stretching a string from the inside edge of any out-of-bounds stake to the next. Trim all grass around the out-of-bounds stakes to ground level.
- Do not mark (paint) the water hazards or drop circles during the month immediately preceding the tournament.
- Complete the preparation and assembly of all supplies, along with all trimming, by the end of the Monday of Advance Week.

# GENERAL

Keep in mind the following general factors when preparing a course for tournament play:

- If this is a return event, review the previous year's tournament reports, paying special attention to any recommendations or requests made by the Rules Officials and as directed by the Agronomist.
- Have adequate mowing equipment and personnel on hand to completely prepare the course for daily play, keeping in mind that weather can reduce the time to successfully accomplish these tasks before play begins. See the checklist in Appendix A for specific recommendations
- Provide a 5- to 6-foot-wide walkway mowed at either fairway or intermediate rough height from teeing grounds to fairways.
- Fill fairway divots before and during the tournament using approximately a 50/50 mixture of sand and loam soil, sometimes combined with compost or some other suitable organic amendment; do not use 100 percent sand.
- Prepare for rain. Have at least 8 roller-base squeegees on hand and a minimum of 4 mechanical pumps in good working condition.
- Obtain a Hole-in-White applicator and enough paint to paint cups. This is now done for all 18 holes on a daily basis.
- Make certain that all vehicles connected with the tournament (concessions, TV, etc.) have received approval from the course Superintendent, in coordination with the Rules Official, to use the routes to their destinations. This is especially important if wet conditions are present.
- During tournament play, allow the use of electric carts only by the maintenance staff for transportation on the course.

# INDEX